SACRED STONES

God's Principles
for Building a Loving,
Secure and Prosperous Family

—New York Times Bestselling Author—

Master Prophe
E. Bernard Jord

FOGHORN
PUBLISHERS
"Of Making Many Books There Is No End..."

Sacred Stones: God's Principles for Building a Loving, Secure and Prosperous Family

All Scripture quotations, unless otherwise indicated, are taken from the Holy Bible, New International Version® NIV® Copyright 1973, 1978, 1984 by International Bible Society, The King James Version, and the Amplified Version. Used by permission.

Sacred Stones: God's Principles for Building a Loving, Secure and Prosperous Family

Zoe Ministries
310 Riverside Drive
New York, NY 10025
212-316-2177
212-316-5769 fax

ISBN-10: 1-934466-07-7
ISBN-13: 978-1-934466-07-0
Printed in the United States of America

Foghorn Publishers
P.O. Box 8286
Manchester, CT 06040-0286
860-216-5622
860-568-4821 fax
foghornpublisher@aol.com

Prophetic Partners

I would like to thank each of these prophetic partners for sowing a seed toward this book. Their financial seeds have made it possible for you to be able to receive this book without charge to you. May God add life to every giver, for through your gift you are causing life to perpetuate in others.

Ramnarine and Patricia Petybaboo

Millicent Raglan

Regina Croswell-Turner

Robert and Brandi Meola

Basil Gibbs

Stephanie Mitchell

Padarrah and Wanda Moss

Garrett Ucheya

Mark and Laurie Hicks

Robin Morgan-Matthews

Derek and Autumn Gabriel

Evelyn L'Elie Davis

Terrance and Willie Mae Parris

Shawn Sipp

Rhea Coleman

Donald and Gloria Kelley

Sandra Dixon

Table of Contents

Introduction

A God of Generations

SACRED STONE #1

Family is the extension of God on earth.

Who do you come from? Who will your children's children be? If you are like most people, you think of your family in terms of your *immediate* family—your wife or husband, your children, your parents and brothers or sisters. We focus on what is here and now, on the seeds we plant today. But while we stand here on Earth today gazing at the seed in our hands, God is already looking at the fruits that will come forth from that single seed. God has already seen the harvest. He already knows how bountiful we can be when we procreate in His name.

This book is about family—what it is, what it means, and the sacred charge God has given us in building and nurturing our families. Family has many meanings to many people, but it has only one meaning to God's people, those who have been reborn in Christ: family is the extension of God on earth. We must grow and maintain our family structures in accordance with certain guiding principles that God has set down. I call these principles "Sacred Stones," because each is part of the foundation of a sound, loving, joyful, productive family that will enhance not only its own life, but the lives of all for many generations.

We must learn how to take the seed that God has given us and wrap significance around it. Our seed determines our future. If we take that seed and throw it away, or we plant it but don't give it the care and attention it needs to grow and thrive, we waste it. When we waste our seed, we waste our future. But when we nurture that seed and cultivate it and give it everything it needs, we give life to the future. We enable our seed to reach the fullness of its purpose: reflecting its creator.

Just as dogs beget dogs and cats beget cats, God begat God. God did not change the order when it came to man. God is always begetting himself. Just as Adam was formed in the image of God, we were created in His likeness to demonstrate the kingdom of God. This is true of our children, our children's children, and so forth for all the generations to come. It is only through the realization of our true identities in Him that we will experience the liberating power of Jesus Christ. Once we understand and accept this, we win in the game of Life.

Your Family is God's Family

SACRED STONE #2

Each of us is the expression of God in this world, and each of your children, even those yet unborn, are an expression of God and of you.

Each of us is the expression of God in this world, and each of your children, even those yet unborn, are an expression of God and of you. We are all many generations removed from God and no generations removed at the same time. There is an unbroken line between the children playing in your house as you read this book and the Creator as He created the heavens and the earth.

Of course, it is not enough to be born into the family of God. That is but the beginning. We must realize that birthright to its fullest potential, and for that, God can only guide us. We are free to choose how we bring our family to fruition—how we and our spouse communicate, what lessons we teach our children, what our family unit gives back to the community and the world as a whole. This is a challenging time to raise a family. Morals are called into question. Traditional values are under assault. The Internet opens children up to new worlds of peril. As such, it becomes more vital than ever before that we as adults and the chosen of God learn the sacred principles behind building a strong, loving, just, and holy family.

We must be the guiding lights for our children, the role models and mentors that lead them down the path of good—indeed, down the path of God. This is not an easy task, and that is why so many of our children have strayed so far from that path. Money problems, lack of a strong father in the home (or any father in the home, for that matter), failing to set boundaries, failing to praise the Lord— these are just some of the things that have led our families astray. Men and women become parents long before they have even become adults. Physically they are mature, but emotionally and intellectually they are not. They are focused on what they want and not what they must give. As a result, we have children raising children, and we have no strong, mature adults to lead us into the future.

Putting Ourselves to the Test

SACRED STONE #3

It takes a congregation to raise a child according to the principles laid down by God.

God is a god of generations. He looks to us to celebrate the giving of life and the raising of our children to reflect His image now and in the years ahead. In this book, we will explore the tools needed to build a strong foundation for the family and learn how to recognize and understand the challenges our families face in our world. We will learn how to overcome them to build strong, spiritual families that reflect the Lord and reach their potential in God.

There is no test required to become a parent, no set of prerequisites you must pass. We expect people to overcome numerous obstacles to get a license to drive a car or earn a college degree, but for the most important job in existence, anyone with normal fertility can qualify. This must change if our society is to thrive and if we are to achieve the full potential God has placed within us. We must become both the students and instructors in a master class in nurturing strong, solid, godly families. We must learn the key principles ourselves, pass them on to our children as we bring them up, share them with our adult children, aunts, uncles, cousins, nieces, nephews and the children of our friends. If it takes a village to raise a child, it takes a congregation to raise a child according to the principles laid down by God. We must become that congregation.

Sacred Stones

In this book you will find numerous Sacred Stones. These guidelines and lessons will empower you to:
- Create a strong, secure foundation for your family
- Structure your family according to God's plan
- Raise your children to be responsible, spiritual, and strong
- Create a place for God in your home
- Strengthen your bond with your spouse
- Develop financial security
- Leave a legacy for future generations

The Sacred Stones are timeless. Their lessons were true 100 years ago for my great grandfather, and they are true today. So although we live in an age of *American Idol* and rampant sexuality, of recreational drug use and MySpace, of video games and Internet pornography, the lessons and wisdom of the Sacred Stones will serve as sound, unerring guides to you in your quest to build a relationship with your spouse that is loving, respectful, productive and enduring. The wisdom will lead you toward teaching your children to work hard, to practice spiritual and material discipline, and to approach the milestones of life when they are ready for them—not before.

It is all too easy to throw up our hands when we see the actions of today's parents and today's young people—to give up and assume the current generation is hopeless. But to tell the truth, our parents thought the same thing about our generation, and their grandparents were sure that our parents' generation was bound for Hell in a hand basket. Every generation is inexplicable to the one that came before. It's almost a law of nature. But that does not grant us the right to give up on today's young people or assume our own children will somehow find their way and that there is nothing we can do about it. We can do EVERYTHING about it. Children need parents. Husbands need wives. Wives need husbands. Society needs strong families. And God needs us to fulfill His plan; He needs us to complete His work by carrying out His will in the physical world. We are Spirit made flesh, and when we bring children into the world we birth them as Spirit first, then as flesh. We are all beings with a divine legacy to uphold.

Discover Ancient Wisdom

Some of the advice in *Sacred Stones* may turn you off. This is not a politically correct book; it does not place men and women on equal levels, because God did not. God gave men and women distinct roles to play in the family. He did not make them equals. So feminism doesn't have a place in this book. Prepare yourself for a journey back to the ancient traditional wisdom about the nature of the family;

wisdom that if rediscovered, will help us rescue the family from these desolate times.

Join me on this journey toward healthier, more joyful, more prosperous, more giving families that make the world a brighter place for everyone, and truly fulfill the promise passed down to us by God.

1

The Father

"...*Children are a gift from the Lord;
they are a real blessing...*"

—Psalm 127:3

SACRED STONE #4

*God intended for us to come together
and form families.*

God meant for us to come together and form families. There are very few things that we can be sure God *intended* for men and women to do. We can become lawyers, but we are not born with the knowledge of the laws of justice implanted in our brains. We can paint beautiful masterpieces, but God did not put us on Earth already clutching paintbrushes in our tiny hands. We have to read law books and learn how to paint. Most of the things we do in life, we must learn to do. God did not implant the knowledge within us, within our DNA.

But we *know* that God intended for us to become families. He would not have designed a woman to carry eggs and carry a growing child in her womb if those eggs were not meant to be fertilized. He would not have given men seed and the desire to procreate if that seed were not meant to fertilize the woman's eggs. Women would not be able to produce milk, the only food a young baby needs, if women were not supposed to take on the honor and responsibility of motherhood. We come into this life with everything we need to have children because that is what God intended for us to do. Indeed, that is what He commands us to do:

God blessed them, and God said to them, 'Be fruitful and multiply, and fill the earth.' —Genesis 1:28

When strong men and strong women join together to procreate and start a family, you have an incredible team that can accomplish much in the kingdom of God. Think about the word procreation. PRO-CREATION. Marriage is all about creating, about growing. When it is conducted in a way consistent with the laws of God, a marriage produces a family that can change the community and change the world. Families are the genesis—literally—of the good that flows through this world.

Some will say that even though we come into this world with the physical capacity to create children, we do not arrive here with the mental and emotional capacity ingrained within us. I say that is false. God has given us all the natural abilities we require to be wonderful, loving, strong spouses and parents—if we listen to the voices within us and if we come to marriage and parenting at the right time. Too often today, we have people marrying too young and women becoming pregnant too young because they were irresponsible about their sexuality. That does not serve God. Becoming a parent too young does nothing but blight the lives of the parents and create innumerable obstacles for the children: parental neglect, poverty, ignorance.

Listen to the Inner Parent

SACRED STONE #5

We have all the knowledge we need
inside of us to be wonderful parents.

We have all the knowledge we need inside us to be wonderful parents. We know in our souls how to love children, to teach them, to discipline them, to share the knowledge of God with them. But we get so caught up in the things of this world and the conflicting advice we get from books, TV shows, friends and family that we forget the simple truths about parenting that come from God and live inside each of us:

Love your children above all.
Teach them right and wrong.
Teach them to do unto others.
Teach them to love God.
Teach them to obey rules.
Teach them to rise above obstacles.
Teach them to be independent.

SACRED STONE #6

Marriages without children fail to grow
into the fullness of what God intended.

We all know these things. But we can make ourselves forget, just as we can forget the fundamental truth that we were placed here by the Lord to be parents. When a woman says she does not want to be a mother, or a man says he does not want to father children, this is a sign of a problem in a marriage. Why would a woman decide not to procreate when God has put the eggs for her future children inside her? Why would a man not want to reproduce himself with the seed God has given him and carry his name into the future after he has died to this earth? Why do couples not want to join together to multiply each other?

If you have a spouse who will not multiply you, you have an unfaithful spouse. This is part of the reason so many of our marriages are in danger. The man or the woman, or both, are not willing to follow God's plan and create new life in the name of the Lord. Marriages without children fail to grow into the fullness of what God intended. You should intentionally be pro-creating in your marriage. If you are not, perhaps you are not with the right partner.

God created man in His own image. In God's image He created him; male and female He created them. —Genesis 1:27

The Bible tells us, "God created man in His own image." Not just male man, but all mankind, male and female. The very first family, Adam and Even and their sons Cain and Abel, were all created in God's own image. Every family since then and every family we know today is descended from that image.

Why did God create the first family? Why did God create you? Why did God create humanity in the first place? I'm about to tell you why, and it might blow your mind. Here it is:

We are here to be God's proxy on earth.

SACRED STONE #7

We are here to be God's proxy on earth.

God manifests Himself through us. God cannot accomplish anything on this material plane, because God is pure Spirit. So He created us to be Himself pressed out into this reality, so He could then teach and guide us to accomplish the things He can only do in Spirit. You, I and all of us are God in form, the matter of the cosmos made conscious to regard itself and discover God's purpose. If you don't know that you are God in form, then you are misinformed. If you are misinformed, you live a life of error.

When you understand you were created in the image and likeness of God, and you understand that the children you produce are created in the image and likeness of God, you understand that you have a responsibility to manifest the spirit of God. God has given you the task of raising your children to make God visible on Earth. Are you ready to handle that task?

The Father is God's Voice in the Family

And so we begin our look at the family with the father, the cornerstone of the family structure. It is popular these days to place the father and mother on the same level, to position them as co-equal partners in the governance of the family unit. That may be politically correct, but it is neither socially nor spiritually correct. As the Bible makes clear and millennia of family dynamics confirms, the father must be and is the head of the household. The reason is simple: the father is the representative of the Father; he is God born out into that family unit. While that implies great power, it also mandates great responsibility. Indeed, it is on the father's actions and wisdom that most families will either succeed or fail.

SACRED STONE #8

The father is the representative of the Father; he is God born out into that family unit.

Traditionally, fathers have been the protectors of the family unit. In times past, that may have meant literally protecting his wife and offspring from physical dangers: wild animals, storms, marauding tribes and so on. In our modern age, those perils are rare or nonexistent, so the father now is charged with protecting his family from a different set of dangers: financial insolvency, political upheaval, legal trouble, drug use, crime, and so on. The threats may have changed, but the role of the patriarch is still the same: to look out over the landscape, see possible dangers, and act to protect his family from them.

The father is also the spiritual leader of the family. Since each family unit is ordained and sanctioned by God, the family must make a place within itself for the love, worship and teachings of God. The making of that place and the maintenance of the family's relationship with the Creator is the charge of the father. He is priest, pastor, shaman, monk, teacher, confessor and healer within that tradition. It is every father's duty to nurture and build the spiritual edifice of his family until his children have come into their adulthood, when they can go into the world and discover their own spiritual truth and their own relationship to God.

But fatherhood is not simple, as any father knows. It is not as biologically woven into the fabric of men's being in the way that motherhood is woven into a woman. We do not carry the child within us. We must learn to become a father. And that is the first of our fatherhood Sacred Stones.

SACRED STONE #9

Fatherhood is an office that must be entered.

The office of fatherhood is not entered into simply because a man has a penis and can fertilize a woman's egg. That ability does not mean he has the strength of character to raise children. In many cases, a man's body may be mature, but his mind and emotions may still be very immature. A penis does not make a boy a man, and a child does not make a man a father. The biological ability to father a child and the ability to be a father, with the love, maturity, sacrifice and foresight that it requires, are completely different aspects of our humanity. They do not always go together.

The office of fatherhood must be entered into through the forces of the natural ordering of life. In other words, before he can become a father, a male must pass through five stages, each of which comes with a different mindset, different actions and different desires:

Stage One: Malehood

At birth, a male is simply a person who is male because he has a penis and a "y" chromosome. He is ignorant of any thought of duty or destiny; he only wants to have his most basic needs met, like food, clothing and shelter. This is a very selfish stage, but that is to be expected at this age.

Stage Two: Boyhood

Starting between ages two and three, a male begins to enter a state of self-discovery. His needs become more defined. He is learning to take responsibility for himself, but he is not yet taking on responsibilities for anyone else. This is the critical developmental stage where a young male will learn the basics of what it means to be a man: character, honesty, integrity, keeping your word, fairness and discipline. It is each father's responsibility to pass those lessons down to his son.

Only a father can teach a boy how to be a man.

Stage Three: Manhood

Around age 12, the ego emerges as the boy enters adolescence. The boy begins to feel the responsibilities of manhood. He starts to express the qualities God and his parents have placed in him, and he wants to become someone. He begins to have a vision for who he is and who he wants to become—a vision of career, service, and his future. At this point, he needs the help of his father to become the individual he is meant to be. Jesus was preaching to the elders in the temple at age 13. He already understood his mission.

This time is filled with pitfalls—new sexual awareness can and does lead to premature fatherhood, experimentation with drugs can lead to tragedy or prison, peer pressure can take a young man off the sacred track. Fathers must wield a firm guiding hand during this period, which can last anywhere from six years all the way to age 30. There is no way to predict.

How will you know when a young man has become a man, ready for the responsibilities of family? When he begins thinking about the needs of others before his own needs. Until then, let him sow his wild oats, so long as he does it responsibly! No father can control the path of his son, only guide. Do not force your son to live your dream; he has his own dreams, sent to him by God.

Stage Four: Husbandhood

SACRED STONE #10

Being a husband is a balancing act of giving as much energy to help your spouse live her dreams as you give to your own.

A man who is ready to enter husbandhood has arrived, for the first time in his life, at a place where he can take responsibility for a wife and enter into a union with her. Marriage is a huge leap into destiny. For the first time, the man is ready to put the needs of another on the same level as his own needs.

It is important to address this idea. Many people will tell you, "No, you must be willing to put your spouse's needs before your own." This could not be more false. You cannot live a happy, fulfilled life and build a family that serves the will of God by burying your own God-given desires and hopes for the sake of someone else. A husband cannot live only for his wife, no more than a wife can only live for her husband. You must share yourselves, simultaneously becoming one while still retaining some of your individuality. No man should give up all of his dreams for his spouse; that stunts the soul. Of course, some dreams must be delayed; if you dreamt of hitchhiking across the U.S. with a tent on your back, chances are you'll have to put that on hold if you're going to marry a decent woman who wants a roof over her head. Being a husband is the balancing act of giving as much energy to help your spouse live her dreams as you give to your own. A man must always remain a man, growing and striving.

Stage Five: Fatherhood

SACRED STONE #11

Fatherhood requires maturity, wisdom, care and calmness of spirit that most men take years to achieve.

It is essential for a man to achieve and master all four stages before he enters into the stage of fatherhood. Fatherhood is the epitome of manhood. Fathers, you take dominion over your home and family, providing for them and their future. Your family looks to you for guidance and security, and trusts in your wisdom and ability to manage your family's affairs.

As a father, you are a creator, in the mold of God. You are bringing life out of nothingness, creating a new human being in God's image out of thought and love. That carries within mind-boggling responsibility. That is why fatherhood must only come when a man is ready to deal with the disruptive changes that come with the entry of a child into a household. Suddenly, you must deal with childcare, education, teaching, discipline, and a host of other matters that you have never known before. Fatherhood requires maturity, wisdom, care and calmness of spirit that most men take years to achieve. But the rewards are without peer.

The Qualities of Fatherhood

Do fathers come with certain qualities that mothers do not possess, and that even other man who are not yet fathers do not possess? Yes. These are some of the qualities granted to good fathers by God:

- Foresight—A father must be able to look beyond today's needs to see what must be done to ensure his family's security and well-being years and decades into the future.

- Reason—A father must be the voice of rationality when all else is filled with emotional turmoil. The father must be the one who brings the discussion back to the facts, and determines when the discussion is over.

- Calmness—A father must be above the fray. He may have his own emotional reaction to something, but he must set that aside in order to be an impartial judge of what is right and wrong.

- Order—The father enforces the laws of God, the laws of the family and the rules of the household. He is judge and jury and metes out reward and punishment according to his wisdom.

- Spirituality—The father must possess an understanding of the nature of God's relationship with man, the importance of prophecy, and the need for regular prayer and meditation.

No father is born with these qualities. We all must develop them over time, hopefully learning from our own fathers what each quality entails. That is why a father is essential to any household. A fatherless household is not a family at all. It is an amputee.

SACRED STONE #12

Men have a responsibility to control their sexuality.

Sacred Stone: Men have a responsibility to control their sexuality.

The idea of fatherless households leads directly to this stone. Too many young men do not respect their own sexual power or the sacred nature of female sexuality. Instead, they give into the baser nature of their flesh, of their raging hormones, and they spend all their time trying to find new sexual conquests. For young men of little conscience, this is easy; they cannot become pregnant, so they do not have to live with the consequences of their irresponsible actions. But their female partners do, and more important, so do the children their adolescent couplings produce.

Sexuality is a gift from God, and it is the duty of every man of any age to respect and control his sexual nature until he is in a place in life where he can father children with a spouse with whom he will share his life. The sex drive is very strong, but God placed it within us so that we would be eager to produce children with our mate, not go around sleeping with every woman we can entice into bed. As men, we must exercise greater responsibility.

SACRED STONE #13

The man is the planner, the builder, and the creator of the future for his family.

The bearing of children defines women. Women are sources of life. Life springs from their loins as it sprang from the Mind of God. Women are nurturers, healers, menders, muses. Men do not share this blessing, so we define ourselves in a different way. Men build. Men create. Men conquer. There is a reason that most of the world's entrepreneurs, explorers and inventors are male: we are driven by our DNA and the imperative God placed within us to discover, to make, to forge, and to create something out of nothing. In much the same way as a woman brings forth a child from nothing, men create businesses, nations, books, political movements and technologies from thin air simply by manifesting them according to the laws of God.

So the father is naturally the one who builds the infrastructure of the family: the finances, the services, the house itself. Men plan for the future, research important information, and create solutions to family needs. That is our nature. If the house needs improvement or expansion, it will almost always be the man who makes the plan, finds the needed contractors, and supervises the work. The mother will focus on caretaking, decorating, feeding the workers—doing the work of the heart and spirit. Men focus on the flesh, the future, the need to progress forward. The spirit of God the Creator, who made the heavens and the earth, is very much animated in every male. If God were human, He would no doubt be a tireless entrepreneur.

SACRED STONE #14
Man is not complete without his wife.

For all his strengths and the sacred role given to him by God, man is only half of the family equation. Any husband and father must have a wife and mother to provide balance, the yin to his yang. A man's wife brings the healing, the ancient wisdom, the gentleness, the emotion, the nurturing and the beauty to his life and to the lives of his children. In the same way, the man brings his qualities of strength, honesty, order, and protection to the woman's days. One is truly not complete without the other.

In the end, man and woman are not complete without one another. Each can provide guidance and care for the family in a way the other cannot. When a man tries to be too much like a woman or a woman tries to be too much like a man, the marriage becomes fragmented and the family suffers. We must each be what God set down for us to be. Husband and wife are two parts of a whole. It is the holy order for each man to set his sights on finding the good woman who will make him whole and give him the family he was meant to have.

SACRED STONE #15
The father is the cultivator and keeper of the family.

God took the man, and put him into the Garden of Eden to dress it and to keep it. —Genesis 2:15

What does this mean? It means that God placed Adam in the Garden of Eden and assigned him the responsibility to cultivate it and care for it. Man is the caretaker of the human family. Just as Adam was given the task of being the keeper and the cultivator of God's garden, a father is the keeper and cultivator of the land where he sows his seeds—his family. The seeds in his garden will grow to become his family, and he is responsible for how that garden grows and flourishes.

As a father, you are a provider. With proper care and nurturing, your garden will be fruitful. It will produce righteousness, peace and joy. If you should fail to provide for your garden, it will become choked with weeds. Pests and predators will invade and your garden will die. How do you know when you see a family garden that is in trouble? You know it—you see marital discord, rebellious children, drug or alcohol abuse, domestic violence, early pregnancy, dropping out of high school, and on and on. The diseases of the untended family are varied and ugly. They are a cancer in our society, because one dysfunctional family can breed as many future sick families as there are children.

If you have six children and raise them to be lazy, abusive or filled with rage and hate, then you will spawn six family units that reflect those same unholy values. Do you see where this can go? Those six families can become thirty and on and on. It's an exponential progression of sadness and misfortune. On the other hand, if you raise children who love God, respect their fellow man, work hard, and live with compassion and integrity, you sow the seeds for many generations of strong families.

God has given you the task of being the principal caretaker of your family and home. God never intended for you to sow your seed indiscriminately. Instead, you must embrace the purpose of your harvest. Thank the Lord for the gift of your seed and for the ability to produce children. Accept responsibility for your children and commit to forever caring for them, loving their weaknesses as well as their strengths, and accepting them with all their imperfections, as God accepts and loves all of His children.

SACRED STONE #16

A father cannot raise a family unless he is a man with a plan.

A man is not ready to be a father until he is ready for the responsibilities of having a family. If he is not willing to take on that responsibility, his family cannot depend on him for anything—to pay bills, make it to work on time, or keep authority in the home.

To raise a family, you have to be a man with a plan. When you are a planner, you make decisions and take actions because you are thinking about the future. You can't go out and buy a hot little two-seater sports car when you have three children at home. Your family needs a man with a plan, not a boy with the toys. You must always be thinking ahead of the game. You must always be asking difficult questions:

"What happens if I die suddenly?"
"How can we afford college for the kids?"
"Will this house always be big enough?"
"What will we live on when we retire?"
"Should I be looking for a better job?"

SACRED STONE #17

Fatherhood is the act of building a fortress around your family.

Fatherhood is the act of building a fortress around your family. This fortress is constructed of sound planning which acknowledges that we cannot know what God has in store for us next week or next year. We alone have the divine ability to look into the future and anticipate what may and will happen, and plan for it.

More important, we have the power to create our futures by deciding what we want for our families and making it happen. If we wish to simplify our lives, live somewhere with better schools or retire early, we can make plans to make it happen. That is the role of the father—to dream bold dreams. The mother then applies a dose of reality and common sense, and together they craft a blueprint for the future.

Boys view responsibility as a pressure and a thief of their fun. They live only for today. Fathers continually plan for tomorrow. Men who seek to raise a family do not strip their future to enhance their present. Fathers understand the consequences of their actions and think about that for which they are striving. They plan for the future and prepare to face the challenges that life is surely going to bring their way. They give up what they might have wanted ten years earlier because it simply is not practical.

Basically, if you fail to plan, you plan to fail. The wise father always has a plan in mind—and if he doesn't have one, he comes up with one quickly.

The Burden and the Joy

I've painted a demanding picture of fatherhood in this chapter. As a father, you are enforcer, pastor, sage and financial guru, giving up your dreams so your children can have theirs. But of course, that's not the whole story. Fatherhood can be a burden but it is also the most sublime joy a man can know, truly a gift from God, the original Father.

The burdens and pleasures of fatherhood blend together to create a mix that is subtle, overpowering and seductive. Being a father becomes your life, and as the selfish boy you once were fades farther into the past, you become suffused with the pride and love that goes with guiding your children and watching them turn into thinking, feeling, progressing beings in Spirit and flesh. There is no greater reward.

Now, let's move on to talk in detail about the other half of this sacred family equation. I speak, of course, about Mother.

2

The Mother

"Adam named his wife Eve, because she would become the mother of all the living."

—Genesis 3:20

SACRED STONE #18

Motherhood is a holy office.

Motherhood is a holy office, passed down from Eve, the mother of us all, and Mary, the mother of Jesus. To many women, becoming a mother, especially after years of waiting, often feels like the fulfillment of their reason for being. There is a reason for this: it is the fulfillment of their purpose for being on this earth. God created woman as the counterpart to man, with a holy, sacred ability: the ability to conceive and bear a child in her womb. Motherhood is the highest, best purpose to which any woman can aspire. It is truly what God intends for every woman, though not every woman chooses to become a mother.

Within each woman—once she does become a mother—is a legacy handed down from Eve and Mary through Jesus Christ: the power to create and nurture life in its earliest form and to bring it forth into this world in physical being. Think about it: each wanted child begins as a thought between two loving, mature spouses. *Let us make a child.* Once conception occurs, that thought gradually takes physical form. A child is thought and love in physical reality! That is astonishing. Only a mother has the power to bring that thought into material consciousness and to birth another soul to God.

But like fatherhood, motherhood these days is in some crisis. Roles are changing, sexual freedom results in more teen mothers who are completely incapable of bearing the responsibility of raising a child, and abortion ends the lives of millions of children each year. To be sure, the decision to end a pregnancy is not an easy one. However, it is more important that we work within the laws of God to avoid the conception of children who are not wanted. Motherhood, like fatherhood, needs to come back to God. That is what this chapter is about.

SACRED STONE #19

Women must guard their sexuality.

Men and women are different. Tell you something you don't know, right? Well, let me share with you a vital way in which they are different. Men have no predisposition to be fathers until they are in their mid-20s, at the earliest. That is, young men don't usually want children too early; God does not allow that desire to mature until young men have expressed their desire to test and challenge and be selfish. Men must learn, gradually, the desire for children and family.

Women, however, begin to feel the urge for childbearing when they enter puberty. Motherhood is built into women at the cellular level, and they feel the desire to know more about children, to hold babies, to nurture and care for something. That is normal and natural. Later in life, when a woman is in her thirties and has not yet had children, she will often feel her "biological clock" telling her she needs to have a child. This is much more than a clock. It is the purpose of God speaking, reminding the woman to fulfill her purpose.

But just because a woman feels the urge to procreate, that does not mean she is ready, especially if she is young. The world is full of young women, some as young as 14, who have had irresponsible sex and gotten pregnant. More often than not, the young fathers are nowhere to be found. So the young woman is faced with having a child while still a child herself and either raising it, perhaps with the help of family, but often being forced to drop out of school, or giving it up for adoption. Either way, the children who rise from such situations face difficult lives.

Women, like men, must be ready for motherhood. They must have a level of maturity that transcends age. Some women are ready at 25; others not until 40. But a woman is not ready to become a mother until she can fill the many roles of motherhood.

The Roles of Motherhood

SACRED STONE #20

The woman is the loving, gentle side of God made manifest.

In a very real way, the mother is the hearth and home. She is the welcoming presence waiting at the door when the husband returns from work or the children from school. She is the part of God that warms and lights the room, brings physical and spiritual nourishment to the family, and heals the sickness or fatigue of the day. While the man is building and creating and protecting, the woman is soothing, growing, warming, and embracing. Women are healers by nature. The woman is the loving, gentle side of God made manifest.

Mature women who are ready for motherhood must fill a variety of roles in the household:

- Teacher—The woman and mother is the one who imparts the lessons, reads with the children, takes the hard knocks of the day and turns them into emerging knowledge for young minds, and sits down at day's end to read the Bible and teach the children about God, Jesus and their role in Creation.

- Healer—Women are natural healers, and mothers even more so. For thousands of years, women have been the midwives, nurses, and caretakers of the sick and injured. Mothers fill that role in the family as well, tending hurts, caring for both children and spouses when they are ill, and healing hurt spirits and wounded feelings with hugs, kisses, gentle advice and timeless wisdom.

- Creator—Men are the creators of great, grand things, but women are also creators of smaller, more personal things. In the home, the mother is the one who helps children write books, paint paintings and invent stories. For her husband, she creates ideas for enjoyment, giving back to the community, and nurturing the spiritual life. Women are musicians, artists, poets and dancers—expressions of God's creative heart.

- Decorator—Women and beauty are inseparable, and so the mother naturally brings greater beauty to her surroundings. She is the one who takes the utilitarian space of a house or apartment and makes it embracing and spiritual by anointing it with color, light, fragrance, furnishings, artwork and decoration. She turns a child's room into a wonderland and an adult sleeping area into a temple where she and her spouse can experience God's voice in dreams.

- Keeper of the Hearth—The woman and mother is the master of the kitchen, the heart of the home. She cooks the food, serves the meals, makes sure everyone eats right, entertains and sometimes even tends the garden and grows the food that the family eats. She radiates hospitality.

- Peacemaker—Conflicts arise in any family, but while the man is the enforcer of the rules of family and God, the woman tends to be the mediator. She is the one who calms and helps people find middle ground if it can be found. She cools anger and suggests solutions, especially important with older children who are struggling to find their own identities and roles in God's plan while their parents try to guide them.
- Listener—Often, the wife and mother's job is to listen and be the wise counselor for her husband, the confidante of her older children and the all-knowing sage for her younger children when they are scared or angry. Tapping into the flow of wisdom that is always coming from God, she pays attention and cares, which is often comfort enough in an indifferent world.

The Stages of Womanhood

God has charged women with a set of challenging roles to complement her husband. But women, as do men, come into their ability to fulfill those roles gradually. No woman is born with eggs ready to fertilize; her ability to ovulate comes later, when she enters puberty. Each female must walk her own gradual path to the point where she is emotionally, psychologically and spiritually ready to become a mother. She is ready physically long before. The stages of womanhood:

Stage One: Femalehood

A girl is born with the physical components that will eventually enable her to become a mother. Somewhere in her developing brain is the burning desire to bear and raise children, placed there by God. But at this stage, she is not a woman. She is not even a girl. She is a blank slate, female only by biology, in need of nurturing and years of development before she comes into her identity.

Stage Two: Girlhood

The young girl, at about age 3, begins to develop a sense of identity, of "femaleness." She begins to discover that she looks different from boys, that she has a taste for beautiful things, that she is expressive and emotional. She begins to become a person with her own sense of I Am. She is becoming a child of God in the truest sense.

Stage Three: Womanhood

Girls mature faster than boys, so by age 15 or 16, a young girl will know that she is a woman. She will see the effect her freshly minted sexuality has on young men, and she will be testing boundaries. This is both a stage of growth and peril; millions of young women, especially in minority communities, become pregnant each year out of wedlock, often never seeing the fathers of their children again. It is at this stage that a young woman needs the firm guidance of her mother, older siblings, female relatives and teachers to walk the right path toward adulthood and God.

Stage Four: Wifehood

Many women to this day still feel pressure to marry. In many cultures, being a wife is the only role for women. That is not the case in America, but being a wife and mother are still the most important roles a woman can play. So while it is vital that a woman not be pressured into marrying for its own sake, it is critical that she look to develop those qualities that will make her a good wife: judgment in choosing a husband, tolerance, self-confidence, communication, and boundless love. At this stage, a wise, mature woman chooses a life partner, a man who completes her, with the intention of one day raising a family.

Stage Five: Motherhood

A woman is ready for motherhood when she finally listens to the message God has been trying to share with her all her adult life: her life's purpose lies nowhere else but in creating and raising loving, brilliant, spiritual, healthy children. When she listens to that voice, she will feel her "biological clock" ticking and desire to conceive children. With luck, and with open sharing of their desires before marriage, her husband will feel the same way. If he does not, the marriage should be dissolved; no marriage is complete without children. In becoming a mother, a woman becomes who she is. The true nature of her spirit shines through. She truly becomes a complete being in the intent of God.

SACRED STONE #21

A woman without children is incomplete.

We have all known women who either would not or could not have children. Some could not for medical reasons, while others chose not to bear offspring. I submit to you that while failing to bear children is not a tragedy in the eyes of God, refusing to do so is. Some women and men are infertile, and after years of trying simply cannot conceive a child. In that case, wise couples choose to adopt children, and adoption is one of the greatest acts of love any human can commit. In what other institution can you reach out to another being and say, "I want you to become my child forever"? Failing to have children is sad, but it does occur.

However, a woman who chooses not to bear children is tragic, because she is blunting her purpose in the eyes of God. She is saying, "I am more important than you, Lord." She will never be complete. We all know women who have chosen not to have children and at some time in their 40s or 50s been struck by the pain of that decision. Sometimes, the regret and remorse over not becoming a mother can become a true spiritual crisis. Every woman was meant by God to have children, either biologically or through adoption. Every woman holds that part of Mary inside her, the wise, cradling mother tending her children like flowers, bringing them up to beauty and wonder.

SACRED STONE #22

A woman cannot live only for her children.

This can be a controversial point. If God's highest purpose for every woman is to become a mother, how can she give herself to anything other than the raising of her children? My answer is this: God created all of us with multiple selves and multiple abilities, and none of them should be left unused.

The world is filled with women who convince themselves that they must abandon all the other pursuits of life—creativity, starting a business, travel, and so on—in order to devote 100% of themselves to motherhood. And while in the early years of motherhood that kind of total devotion is necessary, it is unwise in later years. God means each of us to do much in this world, and women who are mothers and only mothers can often become bitter and resentful in later life, especially after their children are grown and gone. They feel that they passed up opportunities to express some other aspect of their spirits, to create or build or act or sing.

It is vital that raising children and being a good wife are always the most important aspects of any woman's existence. But they cannot be the only aspects. If you as a woman feel called by

God to volunteer and help others, start a home business or paint landscapes, find a way to do it while keeping your family responsibilities paramount. Balance is the key to much in this life.

The Qualities of a Wife

Just as a man is both father and husband, a woman is both mother and wife. And with that relationship in mind, let me state an eternal truth:

SACRED STONE #23

The most important relationship in any family is between husband and wife.

This is sometimes forgotten. There are women who throw themselves into motherhood with abandon and forget about being wives. This is a terrible error; if any wife neglects her duty to be a wife first for the sake of losing herself in motherhood, she is defying God, and she may well lose her marriage. Her obligation is always to put her marriage ahead of her children. Sometimes this will not be necessary, but if it comes to a choice, the wise woman will choose her husband as the main recipient of her time and affection.

Why? Because the husband/wife, mother/father pairing is the heart and cornerstone of the family. Without them, the family is nothing. The children are branches off the tree, but without the trunk and roots the tree dies. Husband and wife must always put each other first, nurturing and caring for each other, supporting each other in times of hardship or grief and building unbreakable trust. Without that relationship, they cannot take care of their children properly.

A wife brings certain unique qualities to a marriage:

- Emotional understanding—Women tend to have a far greater sense of emotional intelligence than men. That is to say, women usually will understand the source and cause of strong emotions and know how best to deal with them. The wisdom of women in discerning the inner emotional life of others and putting them in a position to thrive emotionally is astonishing. Women bring the emotional resonance to a family in the same way that men bring a sense of honor and integrity to the family.

- Patience—There's an old saying, "Patience is a virtue, possess it if you can, it's often found in woman but it's never found in man." How true. If it was up to many members of my gender, God would never be able to reveal anything to us when we were ready because we'd always been looking at our watches, tapping our feet and saying, "C'mon, Lord, I ain't got all day." Fortunately, women are more patient. They are willing to let things unfold rather than trying to force the action. Mothers are more likely to stand back and let their children make small mistakes, knowing that mistakes are how we learn. Fathers tend to want to "fix" everything.

- Health awareness—As women are healers, they are the ones in the marriage who tend to be aware of and monitor everyone's health. They ensure people get to the doctor and dentist, and that everyone eats right and gets plenty of exercise.

- A mind for detail—Men tend to be big-picture beings. We create grand plans to change the world, but we can be guilty of forgetting about the finer details. Women are wonderful at investigating the details of any situation and reminding men to attend to the minutiae.

- Humility—Men hate to ask directions. Women usually ask directions. The pride of the male is one of our greatest short-comings, but women remind us to be humble in the face of God and His creation. A good wife keeps her man humble without damaging his self-esteem, reminding him that he is but one part of the complete family unit.

SACRED STONE #24

God ordained the man to be the head of the household.

This point seems politically incorrect to many people, but we're not concerned with politics. We're concerned with the sacred duties God has assigned woman and man. One of those duties is for the woman to walk a step behind her husband (metaphorically) and acknowledge him as the head of the household.

This is the case for several reasons. First, the man has historically been the defender of the home and family. Men are stronger, faster and more physically able to defend, hunt, and build than women. That ancient reality persists today, but for different reasons. Today, it's men's emotional strength that puts them in charge. Men are less emotional than women and tend to think in a linear fashion. Women can be emotionally volatile and think in abstracts. So when challenging or important decisions must be made, men will tend to look at them more coldly and objectively, enabling them to make the hard decision.

But most important of all, God has decreed that the woman is the help mate of the man. Adam was created first and given authority over all the earth. Eve was made to help Adam, but there was no doubt who was in charge. God has ordained that the man will be the final arbiter of decisions for the family, the source of wisdom, the voice of reason and deliberation, the judge. In the family, the man is God Himself. It is the charge of every woman to accept this and to empower her husband to be as wise and fair in his judgments as possible.

SACRED STONE #25

Wife and husband complete each other.

This is why same-sex marriage will always be opposed by those who understand God's true work. It is not for some unsupportable moral reason or some misapplied biblical verses. Simply put, God intended woman and man to form two halves of the whole. When a husband and wife come together when both are mature and open, and they both grasp the nature of their relationship with each other and God, they complete each other.

Each brings to the whole aspects that the other lacks; the wife brings her uniquely female qualities while the man imbues his mate with uniquely male aspects. The result: woman and man combine to form a whole greater than the sum of its parts. Each learns from the other and changes with time. If the marriage is healthy and the relationship grows over its duration, they both become greater servants of God than they ever would have had they remained apart.

This is where the concept of the "soul mate" comes in. When two fully realized souls join under the auspices of God, they are like two volatile elements throwing off electrons. They change each other. Great things can occur when a marriage and a family are based upon such a blessed union.

SACRED STONE #26

Feminism is a path to the dissolution of the family.

Many women swear by the importance of the feminist movement to free women from traditional bonds and open up new opportunities for careers, education and beyond. But are we really better off in the post-feminist era? Yes, women should have all those opportunities open to them. But when they come at the expense of the husband and family, more harm than good comes to our society.

Feminism, taken to its logical conclusion, can be the death of the family. It defies the word of God that the primary role of woman is as wife and bearer of children. Feminists want to have their cake and eat it—juggling family, career, personal pursuits and more, as if everything is equal. *Everything is not equal.* Family and husband must come before all other interests. The call to serve one's husband is the most important call any woman can answer, and by casting that call as archaic and even enslaving, feminism tempts women to throw over God's order for their own.

Feminism urges rebellion against the ordained order of human life. In the end, when a woman cannot place her family at the top of her priority list, her relationship with her husband will suffer. The environment in which her children grow up will become unstable. In the end, the family will crack, break and dissolve.

Instead of feminism, I propose that women adopt "familyism" as their credo. Here the needs of home and husband are paramount, followed by the needs of children, followed by the needs of the woman herself. This can require much planning, maturity and discipline, but the rewards—a stronger family and a better marriage—are well worth the trouble.

The Meaning of Infertility

SACRED STONE #27

If God does not want a couple to conceive a child, there is nothing that science can do.

Sometimes, children simply are not possible. This is always a heartbreaking occurrence, when a couple spends years and often thousands of dollars trying to conceive naturally, getting fertility tests, going to fertility doctors, taking drugs and getting in vitro fertilization. On some occasions, the woman will become pregnant but miscarry. Sometimes, science can help fulfill God's will. But when God does not want a couple to conceive a child, there is nothing science can do.

God would not want a couple to conceive? That's right. Sometimes God does not choose to bless a man and woman with children, no matter how hard and how long they try and no matter how fervently they pray. There are two reasons for this:

- A pregnancy would result in a child with severe birth defects or would endanger the mother's life.
- The couple is not well suited for each other and would end up raising children in violence, poverty or dysfunction.

If you have not been able to conceive children, ask yourself which of these is likely to be the case. Do you have a history of birth defects of child developmental problems in your family? Did you use drugs? Or has your marriage been in trouble? Often you can find answers in your dreams or meditation, if you quiet your mind and listen for the voice of God.

In this way, not being able to conceive a child is actually a blessing from God. He is trying to tell you something. Either you would be creating a life of hardship and misery for a sick child or you would raise a sick family unit. Often, couples who are having marital problems find that after counseling, prayer and honest communication—rehabilitating their marriage, so to speak—they suddenly find themselves able to conceive, as God gives His OK. In other cases, it's best to end the marriage and let each partner try with someone else. In any case, never ignore the message of infertility.

But What If We Don't Want Children?

Finally, there is the real situation that does occur from time to time, where both husband and wife do not want children. This is rare, but spouses have been known to choose one another for this reason, because they won't be pressured to have kids when they don't want them. But can this ever be right?

Rarely is the answer. Most of the time when a man and especially a woman says he or she doesn't want children, what that really means is "I don't want children RIGHT NOW." But later, who knows? When looking at a relationship where the spouses do not express a desire for offspring, you must always ask if both man and woman are being true to themselves. We often say things to please others, and no relationship creates this desire more than marriage. We want a harmonious marriage. A man says, "I don't want kids," and his girlfriend says, "Oh, neither do I." Five years later, when they're married and her friends start giving birth, she's likely to change her mind.

But what if both man and woman honestly have looked inside their souls and have no desire at all to have children? Is the marriage doomed? This could be a sign from God that the marriage is unhealthy, so some serious time should be spent talking to a counselor or pastor about the issue. More often than not, I find that such marriages are in trouble, even if the trouble is not readily obvious.

But sometimes, a deliriously happy couple simply won't want children. They're selfish and they acknowledge it. They would rather:

- Travel
- Entertain
- Start a business
- Pamper themselves
- Give back to the community.

SACRED STONE #28

Happy marriages are happy for a reason: God approves of them.

Is that counter to the will of God? Not necessarily. God has ordained that the vast majority of marriages should result in children, but you know what? God makes exceptions. Perhaps a union of two people has the extraordinary potential to help others or create positive change in the world... IF there are no children. In that case, God will bless the union. All things are possible, and we cannot know the mind of God.

Happy marriages are happy for a reason: God approves of them. Now, let's take a closer look at the structure of the family.

3

The Structure of the Family

And God said, Let us make man in our image, after our likeness: and let them have dominion over the fish of the sea, and over the fowl of the air, and over the cattle, and over all the earth, and over every creeping thing that creepeth upon the earth.

—Genesis 1:26

Just as Adam was placed in the Garden of Eden to exercise dominion, fathers have dominion over their family. However, you are infused only with the divine right to exercise dominion. You have to take it; it is not given to you. It is not automatic. At the same time, mothers have their roles to play as well: as helpmates to the father, empowering him, supporting him and enabling him to make sound leadership decisions.

In the ideal family, there is a God-ordained structure that prevails, brings everyone into their divine role, and keeps the family harmonious. In this chapter, we will discuss that holy order and how to enact and maintain it in your family.

SACRED STONE #29

The father is the head of the family and brings the family into purpose.

Just as a man brings focus and purpose to a woman by giving her his name on their wedding day, he also brings focus and purpose to his family. This is why it is so important—no, it is *required*—for a man to know his own purpose and identity before he creates a family. A father who does not have focus and purpose for himself cannot bring it to his children. God did not give Eve to Adam until Adam knew what he had to accomplish and was busy achieving his goal. When his purpose was defined, God created Eve, thus giving Adam the means to start a family.

SACRED STONE #30

The strength of the family is based on the strength of the father.

Like the head brings direction to the body, the head of the family brings direction to the family. A strong family must have a strong leader. The strength of the family is based on the strength of the father. So logically, a weak father will produce a weak family. A good father cannot rely on others to validate his final decisions. He cannot go back on his word. He must be a strong man, not just physically, but intellectually, psychologically and emotionally as well. He must act with wisdom, discretion and consistency, even when what he does is unpopular with the rest of the family. He must take the long view that what may be unpopular today is beneficial for the family in the long run. Remember, the family must endure for decades and spawn a new generation of healthy, God-centered families.

A strong father cannot be a boy in a man's body, because a boy cannot raise a boy (or a girl). Only a man has the strength and maturity to raise children. Only a man has the strength and maturity to be the head. This is why young men who become fathers and marry the mother of their child because they think they are doing the "right thing" are actually making a terrible mistake. There is no easy resolution to a child conceived out of wedlock. But when you place a boy in the position of a man's responsibility, you set him up to fail. A man as a father and husband must have the maturity to act firmly, listen to all sides, show compassion when it's needed, punish when it's warranted, and stand by his decisions.

And while we're talking about heads, let me say that a family can only have one head. I know there are a lot of men and women out there who think you can have a family where the man and woman share all the responsibilities and decision-making. We want to be equals. Our modern feminist tendencies drive us in that direction. But just like a body cannot have two heads, you cannot have two heads in a family. No matter how smart or strong women are—and I know some smart, strong women married to men who aren't as smart or strong—the man has to be the head. That is how God constructed to human family, with each playing their role. Only when that occurs is there harmony.

The Story of Abraham and Sarai

The Bible tells the story of Abraham, who married a woman named Sarai, a name that means "principal one." Abraham was married to a woman who was domineering and took the principal role in the marriage. However, Sarai could not produce any children, so she told Abraham to have sex with her servant Hagar, and they would have a child. Ishmael was born out of this union, and though God blessed Ishmael, God had another heir in mind to spring from the loins of his servant Abraham:

God also said to Abraham, "As for Sarai your wife, you are no longer to call her Sarai; her name will be Sarah. I will bless her and will surely give you a son by her. I will bless her so that she will be the mother of nations; kings of peoples will come from her." —(Genesis 17:15–16)

God changed Sarai's name to Sarah, which means "mother of princes." She then gave birth to Isaac. How did this occur? Abraham took on the role of the head of the household in renaming his wife. He made her subservient to him and changed her orientation in the eyes of God. He brought Sarah into alignment with the divine order of the family. Just as Abraham could not bear and bring to life a child in his body, as that was the role of his wife, his wife could not be the head of the household and the leader of the family. That is the man's role. Once God had shown Abraham the way to realign his family, Sarah was no longer barren and gave birth to the heir from who would spring the line of the Hebrew people.

This is why we have to understand divine order in the Kingdom. A man names a woman at marriage and carries that name throughout the family as the sole head of the family.

SACRED STONE #31

A home without a father has a void that must be filled.

One-third of America's children live in homes without fathers. Two out of five of these have not seen their father in more than a year. This is a national epidemic as dangerous to well-being as any disease. Living in a fatherless household contributes to higher levels of poverty, increased possibility of drug use, a greater chance of homelessness, and increased risk of violent death for young men. Young men without fathers at home are more likely not to graduate high school and more likely to get involved in crime, while fatherless young women are more likely to become pregnant young and live on welfare.

The father is the family's compass, the guide through the trials and tribulations that can come to us in this life. More important, he is the moral center for the family, an example by his actions for his children of how to deal with others, how to keep one's word, how to recognize productive versus destructive people, and how to handle morally and ethically ambiguous situations. Without that strong moral center, families waver, leave the path of righteousness, and fall into chaos and self-destructiveness.

Scripture is brimming over with God's concern for the fatherless:

Father of the fatherless, and a judge of the widows, is God in his holy habitation. —(Psalms 68:5)

Defend the lowly and fatherless; render justice to the afflicted and needy.

Rescue the lowly and poor; deliver them from the hand of the wicked. —(Psalms 82:3–4)

Conversely, there is nothing in scripture about God's concern for motherless. If the mother is removed from the family, there is still direction and authority, and the father can provide nurturing as well. But if the father is removed, the mother steps out of nurturing role and now has to do a balancing act as nurturer and enforcer. Mothers, I know you are strong, anointed and appointed. I know you love your sons but you cannot raise them alone. It is not in a woman's image to make a man. When a single mother makes a boy, there is no one to teach that boy how to be a man. There is no one who has walked the path of developing manhood who can show the boy by example how to respect women and how to respect himself. It is no wonder, then, that many young men raised in fatherless households end up becoming abusive to women.

Absent Authority Equals Absent Character

SACRED STONE #32

When there is no father in the home, there is no respect for authority.

When there is no father in the home, there is no respect for authority. A 25-year study found that young men who grew up in homes without fathers are twice as likely to be arrested and imprisoned. Children from fatherless homes also have higher rates of teen suicide, substance abuse and neglect. The reason is quite simple: without the father to hand down discipline and enforce the rules of the family laid down by God, children grow up with no awareness of consequences. They come of age thinking that the rules do not apply to them; they can do whatever they want. They soon discover, to their dismay, that that is not the case. God holds all to His standards.

For a family to be well, the office of fatherhood cannot be vacant. If there is no authority in that office, kids run into the other officer—the law enforcement officer—and end up in trouble with the law. This is why so many of our communities are in trouble, and so many of our kids turn to gangs. When gangs form within a community, it reflects the lack of father figure. Boys who are denied the father role model will start looking for leadership and mentoring among their peers. Every street gang is a family gone twisted and sour by the needs of young men searching for inclusion, for a purpose and acceptance from other males. Gang leaders become older brothers. The sometimes brutal gang initiation rituals become perverted versions of the horseplay that fathers and sons normally engage in.

However, a boy cannot bring another boy into maturity, and gangs have no understanding of the many dimensions of fathering. Gangs possess an embryonic concept of strength, power and ethics—a warped code of honor that brings a deformed sense of belonging, accomplishment and affirmation that satiates a deeper hunger within the youth that should be satiated by the father.

The father raises sons who become men and is the link to each stage of a male child's growth and development. Beginning at the age of 12 (if not before), boys must have that strong male identity and role model in their lives. If the father is not present, there must be another strong male presence in the boy's life, such as an uncle, Boy Scout leader, coach or church father. Men can take an active role in the church to help a boy in the house of the Lord who does not have a functioning father.

Fathers, you are desperately needed in every community to lead the developmental transition from boys to men. Boys cannot become men without someone to lead them through the process. And this process continues even after they have become adults. Even adult men join clubs where they can be mentored and guided to become better fathers, more successful in their career, and closer to what God wants them to attain. There is always the need for a guiding light.

How Matters Are Resolved in the Father-Led Family

When a father sits at the head of the family, there is a pattern and an order to how the daily matters of life, large and small, resolve themselves. That order will look something like this:

- Someone—the mother or one of the children—brings up an issue that requires decision making and resolution. Often, this takes place at the dinner table, the family's place of communion with each other. A problem is presented, the options are discussed, and grievances are aired. At this stage, the father usually just listens, offering advice or guiding the discussion when necessary. The mother is more involved, coaxing people to communicate.

- The father decides when the conversation is over. He will probably not make a judgment on the spot, preferring to ponder the matter and gather more information, perhaps consult with his wife. But he determines the parameters and duration of the discussion. When he says it's over, it's over.

- Very often, the father and mother will talk quietly in private about the issue, discussing their past experiences and their own perspectives on the situation. This conversation is none of the children's business; it is a private time between husband and wife that the children deserve no part of. During this time, the mother will offer her wisdom and the father will receive.

- Finally, the father will process all he has heard and learned, perhaps turn to God in prayer or meditation for guidance and strength, and he will hand down his decision to the family. This decision will be final, not open to question, argument or appeal. The father is the Supreme Court of the family: his rulings are irrevocable and must be obeyed. He is the ultimate authority below God, God's proxy in each family.

A family's affairs must be carried out in this manner, because this is the path ordained by God and seen time and again throughout the Bible. The children are sources of conflict and disturbances, but that is normal as young people try to find their way. The mother is the wise counselor adding her voice to the father's wisdom. But it is the father who bears the burden and duty of passing judgment. Whether the matter is an increase in allowance or whether a daughter is old enough to date, such decisions can only be made by one person.

SACRED STONE #33

It hurts the family if the mother works outside of the home.

This runs counter to our modern feminist leanings, but God is not a feminist. The concept of set roles in the family—indeed, set roles between men and women—grates on some people. But those people are afflicted with a festering pride that causes them to place their own judgment above God's. That is a colossal error, and it is the reason so many relationships and families have crumbled. God understands the balance that must be maintained between men and women. He crafted it at the Creation.

SACRED STONE #34

Work brings definition to the expression of God within man.

God created man to work. Work brings definition to the expression of God within man. The lack of work in a man's life is contrary to the image and the nature of God. God's intent was that the male would work and shape the world, create and build. When man creates something out of the thought of his mind, he is fulfilling his role as God, the Creator. Each man is God pressed out in mortal form, a creator in the flesh, able to shape the world through his works!

God gave Adam work before he gave Adam a woman. Man is supposed to have work in his life before the woman becomes part of it. In the same way, the father is meant to be the worker in the family. If you are a father and you are not able to work and produce, how are you going to be able to take care of the woman and children who have been given to you?

The father must be a worker. But it is just as important that the mother NOT be a worker. When the mother works outside the home, there is a "ripple" effect that spreads from the home to the community to all of society. The relationship between the man and the woman becomes unstable because the woman feels she is not getting appreciation and recognition in the home, so she seeks it in the workplace. The family structure becomes unstable because both parents are out of the home, leaving no one there to raise the children. Even the economic structure becomes unstable. It topples under the demands of greedy fathers who want their wives to work so that there is more money coming into the house.

Women have their roles to play in the family, and it is essential that the man work but also respect and cherish the role of his wife and the mother of his children. The woman's primary roles must be to care for the children, teach them, keep them healthy, and attend to the health and well-being of the entire household by providing good food, a clean place to live and clean clothes to wear. The family is a garden that the woman must tend daily. It is every man's obligation to understand the importance of his wife's work and to show her appreciation.

It is God's intention that the father be the worker in the family, and it is a mistake to believe that you can have a strong family when both parents work outside the home. Unfortunately for our families and our society, it is a mistake that far too many families are making, which is why we have so many families in trouble. Yes, when the family is having financial problems it is tempting to say to the woman, "Honey, maybe you should get a job." But that short-term financial help results in long-term damage to the family: children feel neglected, their mother is tired from having to work and then coming home to her normal duties as wife, mother and homemaker, and the home environment suffers. Better to figure out a way to cut costs, ask for help from the church community, or ask God for wisdom about the changes to make in your life, rather that send a young mother to work.

I understand that some women have deep desires for career and business pursuits. But mothers, it is your duty to postpone those needs until your children are grown, off to school and independent. Raising children and supporting your husband are your sacred responsibilities. Graduate school and the job market will still be there.

What Place Does the Mother Have?

SACRED STONE #35

The mother is the life support of the family.

So if the mother must leave work to the father in this God-ordained family structure, what parts does she play in supporting and maintaining the edifice of the healthy, thriving family?

We've already discussed everything from cooking to cleaning to childrearing. But those are duties within a job description. The heart of the role of the mother in the family structure, as set down by God, is as life support. The man, husband and father is the physical structure of the family building, the steel frame, the solid rock that supports the weight of children and mortgage and trials and difficult times. But behind the scenes is the mother providing the stuff of life to what would otherwise be a lifeless building.

If you occupy a building but fail to pump in fresh air, keep it clean, fill it with light and plants and beauty and energy, it becomes stale and lifeless, unable to support those to whom it was meant to provide refuge. The mother's place in the family is to heal, mend, restore and comfort. She brings the vibrant air into the family with her love and caring. She soothes her husband's worried brow and sore body at the end of a long week of work. She maintains the ties with the community and the church. She reaches out to others in time of need with compassion. She does the small things that make the children smile, forget their tears, and lose their fears.

The mother as wife reminds her husband that while he is the judge of the family, he does not know everything. Men, we're familiar with that, aren't we? Most of our women do a wonderful job of reminding us how much we don't know! But seriously, if the man is the rigid, strong, unyielding rock of the family, the woman is the organic, natural, bending, lovely willow tree. Both are needed to create an environment where life can thrive. The mother/wife/woman is the man's link to the spiritual and the transcendent. She reminds him that at the end of the day, there is peace, love, comfort and joy.

SACRED STONE #36

Families are driven by systems.

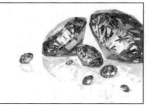

Everything in life is driven by a system. There is a system for buying real estate. There is a system for starting a business. There is a system for staying healthy and for getting better when you are sick. There is a system for creating wealth and maintaining that wealth. To be successful, you must learn how to master these systems. If you don't master them, or the systems break down, you run into problems. You don't get the end result that you want. You buy the wrong house. You end up in the hospital. You find yourself constantly in debt and never able to get ahead.

The family is a system as well—a structured and complex system that, when it runs correctly, produces excellent outcomes. Happy, spiritual, healthy, productive adult children and a happy husband and wife are the products of the system run smoothly. Also, there are many sub-systems in the family. They are responsible for doing things like keeping harmony in the household, making sure the children are behaving, keeping the house clean and well-maintained, paying the bills and so on. The family is an organic, God-centered machine.

As head of the family, the father is the master of the systems, though the mother runs some of them herself. The father is the captain of the ship, the mother his first mate (where do you think the term "first mate" came from?). It is up to the father, along with the mother, to establish the sub-systems that lead to a strong family and a successful future for their children. Whether the system is how to clean up the kitchen after a meal or how to study for a big test at school, you need to raise your children to observe and learn and put into practice the systems of success.

SACRED STONE #37

Wherever there is a system, there is a shortcut.

Here's a very important thing to understand about systems: wherever there is a system, there is a shortcut. A shortcut is a way of trying to go *around* the system to achieve the end goal. You try to avoid the work required by the system, to find a way to do something easier, with less sacrifice. Children are masters at trying to find ways around the family systems! They will test and push the boundaries of every system... and they are supposed to. That is part of maturation and discovering your independence.

However, as parents it is your job to teach children that the system has its purpose. When you try to achieve something without going through the system, that is when the trouble comes. For example, what if your daughter decided that rather than complete tough math homework by working out all the problems, she just copies the answers from someone else. Sure, her paper is right, but what happens when she takes her test later on? She fails, because she didn't use the system to gain the knowledge. She sabotaged herself with her own shortcut.

In a darker example, maybe your son finds out that he can make a lot more money selling drugs on the street than he can working at the local video rental store after school. Sure, for a few months maybe he's making big bucks, but then he gets arrested. SLAM. He goes to jail, maybe. In all likelihood, there go his dreams of college and a great career. When you take a shortcut you get *cut short*. He decided the system was too much work with not enough reward, but he didn't realize something:

SACRED STONE #38

The system is the reward.

Parents, make sure your children understand that *there are no shortcuts*. If you don't respect the system, you can't reap and enjoy the benefits of it. Children think in terms of pleasure and pain; they don't care about "building character" unless you help them care. You need to teach your children that the lessons they will learn in following the systems of your family—discipline, hard work, the ability to overcome obstacles, creativity, and commitment—will give them an edge throughout their lives. It's not the $6 an hour job at the video store that pays dividends; it's the commitment and professionalism to show up every day and do your best.

If your children don't follow the systems of your home, they cannot live in your home. You have to make that clear right away, because when things remain out of order, people learn to live out of order. And that is what brings about the failure—of the system, the home, the family, and ultimately the community. Systems are designed to bring success.

Creating Your Family System

We're almost ready to move on to talking about childrearing. But first, how do you create systems for your family? It's really not difficult. God has set down the things we must do to grow a healthy family. All you've got to do is follow them. The aspects of your family life you may want to create a system for:

- Household rules
- Chores
- Schoolwork
- Friends and playtime
- Dating
- Finances
- Retirement
- Resolving disagreements
- Employment

You may be able to think of others. Create whatever systems you feel your family needs. It's not hard. You just ask and answer some key questions about each of these areas of family life:

- What result needs to occur for the family to prosper?
- What is each person's role?
- What is the right way to create the result?
- What are some of the wrong ways?

- What is expected of each family member?
- What is the penalty for not obeying the system?

With this information, you will be able to craft a set of systems—sort of an owner's manual for your family—that will help you guide them through all of life's rough waters. No system can anticipate the things that happen in life, but having strong systems in place vastly increases your chances of success. And remember, always turn to God for the wisdom to create the systems that do His will. Amen

4

Raising Boys

Teach a child to choose the right path, and when he is older, he will remain upon it.
                        —Proverbs 22:6

The fact that a man and a woman can be parents physically does not mean that they know how to be parents emotionally and intellectually. Too many parents do not know how to give their children the guidance and support they need to grow into responsible, independent, spiritual and emotionally secure adults.

In this situation, raising boys to become responsible, caring men of character and spiritual strength is an immense challenge. Boys show a restlessness that girls don't exhibit; they are bundles of energy and dynamism that reflects their God-given creativity. But that need to be stimulated and to have new experiences can also put young men at peril: experimenting with drugs, running with a bad crowd, getting into crime, even fathering children out of wedlock. Thus the greatest challenge parents face today is to rear young boys into noble, hard working young men who eventually become admirable fathers. Doing so is fulfillment of one of the holiest charges God has given to us.

First, some basic concepts of sound parenting...

SACRED STONE #39

Love your children, but only baby your babies.

All children need love and affection from their parents. Clinical research has shown us that lack of nurturing and affection can actually have an effect on how an infant's brain develops. Infants who do not receive constant touching and affection early in life are less likely to develop strong cognitive abilities, to read and write and do math at a high level. Babies who are cuddled and held and made to feel safe and stimulated with music and reading at an early age are more apt to rise to their full potential, whatever that may be.

During the first year of life, babies are helpless. They have no higher brain functions; they are purely sense-driven creatures who have years before they begin to show awareness of the Self that lies in their spirits. They are driven by their most basic needs: hunger, thirst, sleep and comfort. Since they cannot do anything for themselves, you have to do everything for them: feed them, bathe them, change them, put them to bed, and so on. You have to make sure they have everything they need and clean up after them. Babies are all about instant gratification. When my son was an infant, he wanted *what* he wanted *when* he wanted it. If he wanted a bottle at 1 a.m. and another one at 4 a.m., he got it! Why? Because he was a baby!

But instant gratification is not the way life works. At some point, our babies must grow up and learn to do for themselves. There comes a point when there should be no more nurturing from the mother. Just as child is "weaned" from the mother's breast, he or she needs to be weaned from the mother's influence. Mothers, no matter how experienced, sometimes feel the pull to keep their children young forever, even though this is not possible. That impulse is dangerous; it breeds dependence.

Stop calling your sons and daughters "my baby" at age three.

After a child reaches the age of three, its mother should no longer refer to the child as "my baby." This child is not a baby. This is now a boy or girl. He or she can start to do things for himself or herself. This boy or girl can begin to have responsibilities around the house, be assigned chores, follow rules, accept punishment, and communicate by words, not gestures or noises. As his parents, it is your responsibility to make sure that children at this age start to do things for themselves.

Make Him Independent

This is especially vital for boys. Girls have a biological imperative that's placed in their bodies by God: they eventually want to become mothers. This need is so powerful that it can become all-consuming. As a result, many girls begin at an early age to prepare to become mothers: playing with dolls, caring for pets, and learning about babies. They begin early on to find their purpose. But boys have no such biological coding. A man does not have something in him that says, "You must become a father." This must be learned. And no man who is tied to his mother's apron strings can learn the fortitude, calmness of mind and vigor of spirit that are needed to discharge the duties of the father. You, the parents, must force your sons to find their own way and become their own young men.

In other words:

SACRED STONE #40

*The greatest responsibility any parent
has to a son is to make him independent.*

This may fly in the face of accepted wisdom. Is it not a parent's responsibility to teach his or her son the love of God? Honor? Hard work? Respect for others? Justice and law? Those are all very important, but in order to fulfill God's set role for him, each male must become an independent person and develop those qualities God wants of him.

To be a father at the head of a household means standing alone sometimes, being in the lonely position of making unpopular decisions or going against what your wife or children want in favor of what they *need*. A man who has not developed a powerful, resonant sense of independence cannot make those kinds of decisions. He is too busy seeking approval, trying to make everyone happy. Leaders cannot make everyone happy, and the father is the leader of the family. Your job is to train your boys to be leaders.

No three-year-old child has any business still being in your bed. The only reason he or she should be in the bed is to breastfeed. Once a child is weaned, he should stay in his own bed in his own room. This can be scary for the child, but it is a rite of passage that every child (and every parent) must go through. It is the first step to becoming independent and self-sufficient. The children who do not go through this passage are the ones who are still living at home when they're 30 and having mama do their laundry! Or perhaps they are married and even have children, but are still living off their families. That's a shameful, terrible situation.

Boys must go through this dark period to grow. If they don't learn how to make this transition at age three, they will not know how to make the transition to puberty at age 12 or manhood at age 18. When someone breaks their heart at age 23 or they have problems at work at age 30, they cannot go running back to mama. They have to learn how to face challenging situations on their own. These are lessons that can only be taught within the confines of the family. If your children don't learn them within the family, they will never learn them in the streets.

What Men Must Teach Men

SACRED STONE #41

The main job of the father is to raise his son.

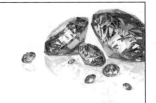

Fathers, you must pick up where your wives left off. You cannot be out playing the ponies or spending all your time at work. Raising your son is your main job. As he starts to grow into himself, teach him. Become his mentor. Test him. Take him to be with other men so he can learn how men talk and share and joke and kid. Teach him the things that men do: hunt, fish, make crafts, play baseball and football. Teach him to defend himself. Teach him judgment and honor. Imbue in him the idea that a man always keeps his word.

Teach him sports and become his coach. Let him fail. Let him strike out or get tackled and learn that the only failure in life is not to get back up after you're knocked down. Share with him some of the ways you disobeyed when you were young: sneaking out of an unlocked screen or making a rope ladder to climb out of the house to read comic books with your friends. He's going to test you, so share the ways you tested your parents. Tell him what books you used to read and learn what musicians he likes. Know where he's surfing on the Internet. Meet his buddies. Be the cool dad but know when to leave him alone. Boys are more solitary than girls and need space to think and reflect and brood. Let him know that it's OK to pursue his passion, whatever it might be.

Make sure he comes to know God. Answer his questions about Jesus and the Bible and the contradictions that some see in religion. Let him know that not everything everyone says about faith and belief are true, and make sure he is aware that the most violent disagreements he will ever encounter will be about religion. Teach him to pray and meditate on the Lord and how to listen to the voice within his mind. Make sure he knows your politics. You don't have to give him a civics class, but talk about government and war and what it means to be free and the responsibilities he has as a citizen of this country.

Give him a job. Make him earn his allowance every week. Set an amount and tell him that he will get a raise when he shows that he can maintain excellence week in and week out. When he is old enough, make him get a job. Go with him to a community center and sign him up to mow lawns, help old ladies with their groceries, or paint houses. He'll grumble and complain, but the money he earns doing this work will be nothing next to the work ethic, determination and discipline he'll develop. You'll be teaching him to appreciate the material things in life, the things he'll be charged with providing for his family someday.

When he's old enough, teach him to drive. Teach him what it means to drink. Tell him not to smoke, to eat right, to take care of his health. When the time is right, tell him about sex and how women become pregnant and instruct him in what it takes to avoid having his life ruined by making a girl pregnant before he is in a stable marriage and prepared to be a father.

The Qualities of Manhood

SACRED STONE #42

The father's job is to put his sons in the position to develop the qualities of manhood for themselves.

In the end, your place as a father is to put your sons in the position to develop the qualities of manhood for themselves. You cannot magically give them those qualities; you can only demonstrate them. God has decreed that we must learn the lessons that shape our characters, and so parents can only give their sons the tools and habits and attitudes to go into the world and become students of manhood.

These are the qualities of manhood you should be preparing your male children to discover and hone:

- Honor, the sense that a man never breaks his word.
- Integrity, the notion that a man treats all others fairly according to how they treat him.
- Spirituality, the love of God and openness to His voice and His will.
- Judgment, the ability to know when people that come into his life are good or bad and to reject the bad ones.
- Discretion, the power to refuse temptation that can pull him off course.
- Work ethic, the knowledge that nothing worthwhile happens without a great deal of hard work and a system; there are no short cuts.
- Discipline, the idea that sometimes he must sacrifice what he wants to do now in order to benefit in the long term.
- Respect for women and his elders.

- Courage to stand his ground against injustice and defend himself when necessary.
- Thrift, the will to save rather than spend.
- Teamwork, the ability to cooperate with others for the greater good.

Show your sons these lessons all their lives; your actions will speak decibels louder than your words. Your sons will learn from what you do, absorb the lessons you teach, and discover these qualities for themselves.

SACRED STONE #43

After age three, men should raise boys.

Many parents don't know this, but boys actually need more affection than girls. Why? Because after a boy becomes a man and gets married, he stops *getting* affection and becomes the *giver* of affection. By nature, a man is the giver of life. That is why men have their sexual organs on the outside. A woman, who receives life, has her organs on the inside. So once a boy reaches manhood, he has to learn to give affection to others.

Wait a minute. Doesn't this contradict what we've already said about the mother being the healer and hugger while the father is the stoic dispenser of justice? No, it doesn't. Fathers are judge and leader, but they are also givers of strength and love and security. A father's affection is different from that of a mother; it is protective and sheltering and commanding. I have had fathers tell me that their most cherished time around the house is at night when their wife and children have gone to bed and the house is quiet, but they are still awake, doing their night business. These fathers feel an over-whelming sense of protectiveness of their sleeping loved ones. In this quiet, that is the voice of God speaking loudly, a Father's affection for His affectionate son.

SACRED STONE #44

A mother should give her son lots of affection and nurturing until he is about three years of age.

Here is the rule: A mother should give her son lots of affection and nurturing until he is about three years of age. At this point, the voices of the father and the men in the community should become louder and louder, until they are the loudest voices in the boy's life. This is the first step in teaching a boy to take his destiny into his own hands, build a strong family and, ultimately, help build a stronger community and a stronger race. Only men can teach a boy how to be a man. Only men can show him by example how to fill the role that God has determined for him as head of the family. This means not only his father but elder brothers, uncles, grand-fathers and friends of the family in the church and community. There is a reason the word "mentor" begins with the word "Men."

If this fails to happen, and the mother continues to be the main influence in the boy's life, he will always want to be babied by his mother rather than becoming a leader and taking on the responsibilities he is meant to have. Have you ever wondered why, when you hear about a 30-year-old person who is still living in his parents' basement and has never done anything with his life, that nine times out of ten it's a man? This is because women are driven to mature by their ability to conceive and carry children. That forces a sense of responsibility on them. Men must learn to be men, and they cannot do it by being coddled by women. Most of the time, such ne'er-do-well men were tied to their mother's apron strings to an unhealthy age.

Mothers, Know When to Let Go

SACRED STONE #45

By the time a boy is 12 years of age, he should start becoming responsible and independent.

Sometimes, a mother will resist when the men start to take over in her son's life. When men begin to discipline the boy, teach him their sometimes rough lessons and set him on the road to becoming a strong man, the mother may protest, "What are you doing to my baby? He's just a little boy!" This is exactly what prevents boys from becoming men who lead strong families. These boys never experience discipline because mama never says "No." This occurs in Italian culture all the time. There, young men traditionally live with their parents until they marry, even if they do not marry until they are 40! I can't think of a more unhealthy lifestyle for mind and spirit. It is this coddling, give-him-whatever-he-wants behavior from women that effectively "neuters" our boys and renders them incapable of becoming men. Instead, they always remain "mama's boys." That's the last thing we need.

By the time a boy is 12 years of age, he should start becoming responsible and independent. He should not need his mother to tell him to clean up his room or take out the garbage. He should be doing that on his own. He should not need to be corrected by his mother; in fact, he should be ashamed at having a woman tell him what to do. Make no mistake, he is still subject to his mother's discipline; he is still her child and living under her roof. But he should not need to receive her direction or discipline.

In fact, after age 12 a boy should not only no longer be taken care of by his mother, but should start to *take* care of her. These are a boy's formative years, and they should be practicing their manhood with their mothers and perfecting it over these years. Then, by the time they do marry and have a family of their own, they have already learned to be men and are not making their "learning" mistakes with their wives and children. This means a young adolescent man should begin doing nice things for his mother without being asked, mowing lawns so he can give her some money for the groceries every week, helping younger siblings with their homework so she doesn't have to, and so on. He should begin becoming the man of the house, second rank, below his father.

Empower your boys to become men. Unless they get that practice in your home, they will not succeed in their own homes. Think of a maturing boy as a bone. Just as a young, pliable bone can be broken and re-set more easily and successfully than an older, harder bone, it is easier for a boy to break a bad habit and learn the right way to do something when he is still growing than when he has reached age 20 or 30 or 50.

SACRED STONE #46

"Smother love" prevents boys from becoming men.

Too many mothers cling to their sons, smothering them with "mother love" instead of letting go of them and allowing them to become men. Because of the high divorce rate in our society today, a lot of young men have become surrogate husbands to their single mothers—not in a sexual way, but in an emotional way that keeps the boy tied to his mother's apron strings at an age when he should be out of the house and preparing to raise children of his own. The mother doesn't want to let go because she still wants a man in the house; on some level, she is emotionally "married" to her son and won't "divorce" him.

One of the reasons new wives have problems getting along with their mothers-in-law is that their husbands were still emotionally tied to their mothers when they got married. Now, mama doesn't want to let her boy leave her for another woman, even if the other woman is his wife! Mama doesn't want to share her place in her son's heart. Besides, she thinks, no woman is good enough for her baby—even if her baby is 6'2" and weighs 220 pounds! I don't have to tell you how unhealthy this is.

SACRED STONE #47

You must learn the sacrifice of letting go, because only that sacrifice can lead to the ultimate reward for any parent.

Mothers, you must intentionally release your sons into manhood. You must understand that there are some things you cannot teach them. There are lessons they cannot learn from you or from anyone. They must go out into the world with the character you have helped them build and make their own mistakes. Their experiences will shape the character they develop as they become men, and will help determine the kind of men they will become.

As a mother, you must learn to change the view you have of your son. You must learn the sacrifice of letting go, because only that sacrifice can lead to the ultimate reward for any parent: the joy of watching your boy grow into a strong, just, good, kind, resilient, fair, wise, loving husband and father, carrying on your legacy. That is the most profound joy any parent can experience, and it can only come when you trust what you have taught them and let them free into the world with God at their sides.

5

Raising Girls

"When a young woman still living in her father's house makes a vow to the Lord or obligates herself by a pledge, and her father hears about her vow or pledge but says nothing to her, then all her vows and every pledge by which she obligated herself will stand."

—Numbers 30:3–4

SACRED STONE #48

Only a woman can teach a girl how to be a woman.

As only a man can teach a boy how to be a man, only a woman can teach a girl how to be a woman. We each offer our own unique perspective on maturation that the other gender cannot match. The problem of young mothers trying to pass along life wisdom to their daughters, when they bear little of that wisdom themselves, is one of the sources of our society's problems. Life's trials—early pregnancies, a mother who was not at home, drugs, poverty—deny many young mothers the opportunity to gain the knowledge that their daughters need to make the transition from girlhood to motherhood. As a result, we are often locked in a cycle of dysfunctional womanhood that affects children, husbands and communities.

Just as God has ordained the progress of how boys become men, He has ordered the rise of young females from infant to the exalted state of mature motherhood. But this is a perilous journey; young women in our society are beset by dangers like early pregnancy, peer pressure, the temptations of their own sexuality, and a popular culture that asks them to grow up too soon and turns young girls into sexual stereotypes. The many land mines strewn throughout the landscape of young girlhood are a major contributing factor to our culture's skyrocketing rate of teen pregnancy and premature motherhood. God requires both mothers and fathers not only to learn the skills necessary to rear strong young men, but to raise wise, caring young women who understand their role in His plan.

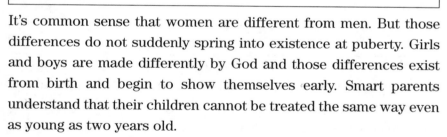

SACRED STONE #49

Girls and boys are made differently by God. Those differences exist from birth and begin to show themselves early.

It's common sense that women are different from men. But those differences do not suddenly spring into existence at puberty. Girls and boys are made differently by God and those differences exist from birth and begin to show themselves early. Smart parents understand that their children cannot be treated the same way even as young as two years old.

- **Girls are verbal.** Boys are very physical as children, constantly lifting, throwing and feeling things to see how they work. It's no wonder that boys tend to become engineers, architects and builders. Girls' physical nature surfaces later, if at all; as young children they will tend to be introspective, readers, investigators. They will speak early, learn their letters early and tend to be more interested in ideas than boys.

- **Girls are empathic.** God has granted females the gift of empathy, that is, tapping into the emotions of others. Where boys can usually ignore another child (or even an adult) who is clearly upset, girls cannot. If another child is crying, they will frequently cry. You as a parent must be cautious about emotional outbursts in the home when your daughters are too young to understand what they are all about. They will key on your emotions and spend their time worrying about them. Childhood for girls should be partially about learning what emotions are and how to control them.

- **Girls are naturally attracted to beauty.** This isn't to say that boys are cretins who only like the ugly, greasy and messy, but let's face it—boys like to get dirty, break things, burn up ants with magnifying glasses, scare smaller kids at Halloween and generally cause chaos. In contrast, girls at a very young age are drawn to beauty: frilly dresses, decorations, artwork, paint, color, nature and more. Not all girls become artists, but all girls have a need to surround themselves with things that are beautiful. It's an expression of their spirit.

- **Girls like order.** As I said, boys and chaos tend to go together like peanut butter and jelly. Just look at the room of any eight-year-old boy; it looks like a bomb went off. In contrast, the room—indeed, the entire sphere—of a young girl is usually organized, with everything in its place. For many girls, order equals beauty. It is vital that parents allow girls to create spaces that reflect this need for order.

- **Girls are nurturers.** This is perhaps the most important feature that sets girls apart from boys. They are the ones who prune and grow the garden that is the family, giving the love and touching and affection and care that allows life to flourish. At an early age, most girls will begin playing with dolls, or if they have them, small pets. This is because the spirit girls are endowed with leads them to rehearse for the time when they become mothers. Fostering this nurturing nature is essential for parents.

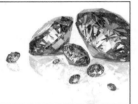

SACRED STONE #50

Boys need challenges; girls need support.

Just as the characteristics of boys and girls are different, so are what they need from their parents as they mature. Boys, even at a young age, seem to need to be challenged to bring out the best in them. They want to run riot through the house; they are bundles of energy. It's no surprise that boys are far more likely to suffer from attention deficit disorder than girls. So wise parents know that they must channel the energy of their sons by posing challenges. The quest to get a job, the household chores, the buying of the first science kit—these are all attempts by mothers and fathers to give their sons obstacles to overcome, knowledge to gain, and goals to reach. The best way to harness excess energy is to find a way to turn it into productivity.

With girls, the needs are not the same. Girls tend to be more sensitive than boys; their feelings are more easily hurt. At the same time, they are calmer and more self-directed; they will often find their areas of interest on their own. When that happens, it is critical that parents give them love and support to let them know they can succeed in whatever they choose to do. Positive statements of confidence, praise for work well done, and even trips to buy books, paints or other tools girls need to pursue their interests go a long way to encouraging girls to become confident young women.

Wait a second? I spend chapters telling you that the most important role for any woman is to become a wife and mother, and now I'm telling you to support her if she shows an inclination when she's seven to be a doctor or politician? Yes, but it's not as dire as that. Remember when you were a child? What did you insist you were going to be when you grew up? Did you become a fireman, police officer or astronaut? And so most girls (and boys) who show an interest in science or business when they are in third grade won't end up being scientists or CEOs when they're 40. Child's interests are just that—childish. But when you offer your sensitive girls support for whatever they do, you give them the confidence to know they can make wise choices, and that is really what this chapter is about.

The other reason you won't have to worry about your unequivocal support for your daughters' interests derailing them from marriage and motherhood is simple biology: God has made all females mothers-in-training. Girls will almost always exhibit a desire to have babies, hold babies, and touch babies. This natural drive to have children and become mothers becomes the most powerful developmental force in a girl's life. Someday, she may have to make a decision about whether career or motherhood will come first, but that is the kind of decision you can help her with, by sharing with her the God-given duty and joy of motherhood and reinforcing her ability to make smart decisions with your loving support. She will choose the right path.

Girls' Choices are More Permanent

SACRED STONE #51

Mothers should teach their daughters wisdom and discretion.

I don't wish to become maudlin or negative here, but picture this in your mind if you would: your daughter at age 25, with three children running around her bare, filthy apartment. There is little food in the refrigerator, and no father to be found anywhere. Your little girl lives on public assistance and her sense of desolation and despair is almost tangible. She feels sometimes that God has abandoned her. You rarely see your grandchildren because their situation makes you want to weep. You want to help her but you do not know how.

Does that sound melodramatic? It shouldn't. It's the true-life situation for hundreds of thousands of young women around this country who were sexually active before they were ready, became pregnant and were forced to raise a young child alone, the father having split the scene. One of the awful truths of such a life is that many young women in this hopeless situation feel that the only way they can get any attention or love from a man is to surrender their sexuality, and so they become pregnant again and face another unwanted child, then another and another. It doesn't take much of an imagination to see how this life would quickly turn into poverty and misery for the young woman and her offspring. How likely is it that her children will grow up to raise healthy families?

Wise parents know that today's young woman lives in peril of losing her freedom to choose, the joys of marriage and love of a good husband, and the sacred beauty that comes from becoming a mother when she herself is a fully mature individual. The peril comes from the simple truth that while even a young man's most foolish choice—the choice to father a child out of wedlock—can be only a temporary setback, for a woman it is permanent. She has to carry the child inside her body and give birth to it. Even if she gives it up for adoption, chances are good she will bear pain and regret for the rest of her life over the child she never knew.

Parents, one of your most important jobs as God's proxies on earth is to educate your daughters in their ordained roles as wives and mothers and to warn them to be careful when they go out into the wide world. Teach them wisdom and discretion. Remind them that there are young men who will speak kindly to them only because of their sexual power. Show them that there is nothing sweet or romantic about becoming the mother of an infant at age 17. Make it clear that you will not, as some families do, raise their child for them if they are so careless as to become pregnant before they are ready to be mothers. It will be their responsibility.

Motherhood is perhaps the holiest of offices. But it is different from parenthood. Anyone can become a parent by virtue of biology. It takes a mature, self-assured woman to be a mother to her children. You must be certain that your girls know the difference between the two and that the journey from parent to mother takes years and will not happen before it is set to happen in the mind of God.

Only A Woman Can Teach a Girl How to Be a Woman

SACRED STONE #52

Mothers should train their girls in the arts needed to run a household and be a good wife.

Like begets like; just as a man is needed to teach a boy to become a man, only a woman can help a girl become a woman. Mothers, past a certain age (usually 5 or 6 years old) you and the other women in your sphere of influence like sisters, cousins, grandmothers and close friends should become the chief influences in your daughters' lives.

At this young age, mothers should begin spending more time with their daughters teaching them how to be ladies, wives and mothers. This time should be spent instructing them on ladylike behavior, discretion and good taste, and how to behave in public. Mothers should be training their girls in the arts needed to run a household and be a good wife: cooking well, keeping a clean house, decorating, tending the garden, mending clothing and active listening. Finally, mothers must begin to acquaint their daughters with the realities of motherhood: how a baby feels, smells and acts, changing a baby, feeding a baby, dealing with a crying child and so on.

This is not all that being a woman is about, of course. But all mothers have a God-given responsibility to give their female children a strong foundation in these essentials. They are the basics that underlie every woman's success in her family life. Example is a far better teacher than any words or formal lessons, so spend time with your daughters. Take them out in social situations with other women whom you trust. Take them to a nursery school and show them how children behave and explain why. When you are out and see a mother breastfeeding, explain why and how she does it and why it is the best way to feed a baby. Encourage your daughters to always dress and act in a ladylike, polite, refined way when in public. When they are at home, let them be children; let them run and jump and play. But girls who learn to be ladies early on in public tend to gain the respect of boys sooner than girls who exhibit coarse behavior.

Give your daughters responsibilities around the house. In the same way that a boy is given chores, girls should be given chores that suit the woman's role. They can help Mom in the kitchen, weed the garden, assist in cleaning the house, fold the laundry and other such tasks. Spend time with them teaching them how to do each task right. Focus on teaching them how to cook and work wonders in the kitchen, since a woman who can cook well and easily for her family will keep her husband and children happy and healthy. Teach your daughters how to keep and have pride in a home and to make it the center of life. This will ensure that her husband remains at home, loyal and loving, and that her children delight in coming home to a place where good food, warmth, love and God preside.

SACRED STONE #53

Fathers must treat their daughters as ladies at a certain age.

The greatest challenge any young woman can face is how to handle the attention of men. Fathers, it is your charge to teach your daughters where men fit into her life by example, and the best way to do that is to gradually draw away from excessive physical affection as your daughter gets older. In fact, after about age seven, you should limit your physical affection to hugs, warm praise and kisses on the cheek. More important, you must not become the stereotypical "give her everything" father who his daughter can wrap around her little finger.

There is a sound reason for both these admonitions. You want your daughter to view men as strong but safe to be around. You are your daughters' model for all men to come in her life. If you give her too much physical affection, it will skew her view of male sexuality later in life. She will come to feel that all men must show their approval of her with intense physical contact. So to protect her in later years, show some restraint. Never fail to give her your love and approval and to tell her she is wonderful, and hug her generously. But also maintain some distance. Fathers must treat their daughters with physical respect, so these budding young women will grow up to accept nothing less from any male. You want your daughters to set strong boundaries for acceptable behavior from men, and that begins with you.

Second, giving a female child whatever she wants creates in her the sense that she can (and should) manipulate men. Make no mistake, she's a young woman; she will already have the power to cloud men's minds. We're weak that way. But it is a mistake to encourage any girl to think that she needs to play games with men to get her way, or that she has the right to get her way all the time. Game playing can backfire and turn into violence or false expectation. Fathers need to arm their daughters with the awareness that men should be handled in a straightforward, honest way that demands and gives respect.

So though you may want to hold your little girl close all the time, as she gets into elementary school, start to create some respectful distance. Give her her space. It may seem awkward to her at first, but after a few years she will want and need that space as she begins to move into adolescence. You will see the difference in her self-confidence, deportment and ability to control any situation—a result of your wise, forward-thinking actions.

SACRED STONE #54

At a certain age, mothers and daughters become peers.

Mothers, you don't get off the hook either when it comes to changing your relationship with your daughters. As your daughters grow up, the dynamic between you must transform. For a few years, your daughter is your baby. Then she becomes your little girl. But starting about age nine or ten, she begins to become a peer with you, a fellow woman. Don't mistake this to intend that you give up your role as disciplinarian; that's not what I am suggesting. However, at some point a young girl begins to think and feel more like a woman, and that is when her mother—her ultimate role model—must begin to treat her as one.

What does daughter as peer imply? Here are some of the possibilities:

*   Telling her about sex—Being a woman implies that a female is ready to find out where babies come from and her role in making

them. At this time, a mother owes her daughter a candid discussion about sex—the mechanics, why it happens, why it's OK to say no, birth control, the whole nine yards. Information is power and you are trying to raise a daughter powerful enough to resist becoming a mother until she is in a solid marriage.

- Including her in social outings—When you go out with other older women, include your daughter. Share the time with her and let her learn how women talk and behave by observing. Let her hear the conversation, share the jokes (even if she doesn't understand them) and manage the social situations. She may have to sit for hours in social settings that are not stimulating for her, but this is a wonderful way to learn to tolerate the interests of others. This is the time she will move from being completely self-centered to a young woman who thinks about others in addition to herself.

- Sharing clothing, when possible—If you're close to the same size, try on each other's clothing. Make it fun. If you're not the same size, share shoes, jewelry or makeup. The key word is "share." You want your daughter to feel a kinship and bonding with you that she feels with no one else. Sharing personal items and turning this into something of a regular ritual can create a powerful emotional bond that nothing else can.

- Letting her know her responsibility toward God—Remember that men and women are both custodians of God's will on earth, bearers of a promise to be Christ's stewards in this reality. Your young daughter must know this. You must sit her down and share with her the responsibilities that you carry out based on God's command, and let her know that she is expected to do the same. This is the time to let her know that her most important duty in life is to raise a family and be a loving, giving wife and mother. Tell her that if she has a desire for other paths she can pursue them, but only until she has a husband and young children. Once that happens, her obligation to God is to give 100 percent of herself to the Lord.

What Parents Must Teach Their Daughters About Men

SACRED STONE #55

Both parents have the solemn responsibility to teach their daughters about their role as it relates to men.

Both parents have the solemn responsibility to teach their daughters about their role as it relates to men. As we have discussed, men and women each have a God-designed role to fulfill in the family structure. To some young women, the ordained roles that God has set down might seem confining and anti-feminist. They are old-fashioned, but ultimately they set the stage for greater joy and fulfillment than any more modern, ways of being.

With that in mind, here are the three truths about which parents must educate their daughters:

i. **What to look for in a man.** There are a lot of wonderful men out there and some bad apples. The last thing you want your daughter to do is select a man who is not willing to fulfill the role that God has set down. You must train her in the qualities that should attract her to a man and the ones that should send her running in the other direction. These are the key qualities of a good husband and father—

- Love of God—The man must have a strong spiritual sense of self, understand his place in God's economy, and be willing to place his own will secondary to that of the Lord.
- Character—The man must be honest and keep his word.

- Financial sense—The man must have a decent job and be able to manage money prudently and with foresight.
- Discipline—The man must be able to resist the temptation of other women and to take care of himself.
- Strength—The man must be confident and powerful in his will, willing to sit at the head of the family and make hard choices.
- Parenthood—The man must have the desire to become a parent and raise children in a home of love, law and Lord.

ii. **How to be subservient to a man.** This does not sit well with many young women, but that is why it's so crucial to explain God's design that the man be the chief executive of the family. The woman is merely vice president—an advisor and confidante, but not the final decision maker. Explain to your daughter the joys that can come with anointing the father as head of the family. Tell her that in this holy order, it is her duty to be the wise counselor, to mediate discussion among the family, to gather information, and in the end to accept and obey the decisions of her husband concerning money, home, travel, discipline, schooling or church. Be sure to emphasize to your daughter that this in no way makes her a second-class citizen to her husband; she is simply fulfilling God's plan.

And mothers or unmarried ladies, if you have somehow forgotten all this, perhaps you can use this section as a refresher course!

iii. **How to manage a man.** Let's face it, we men take some managing. You women know this. We like to go out, we cause trouble, and sometimes we stick our noses into aspects of the family where we don't belong, such as the kitchen or the laundry. Occasionally, our inability to act as the calm mediator and listener causes conflict. We can be bulls in china shops. But we mean well. A wise wife knows this and understands how to manage her man to achieve good results without bruising egos.

What can parents tell their daughters about managing their man? Plenty:

- Remind him about his sacred role in the family. Some men want to do everything, and they can't. Remind him what he's best at and what he needs to let his wife do.
- Be prudent with money. He works hard to bring in the money and needs his wife do spend it wisely. Reckless spending creates more marital conflict than any other cause.
- Praise him when he does well. Everyone needs to be given credit when they excel. When your man buys a wonderful gift, does the dishes or puts together a Christmas gift while the clock is ticking, tell him that he's the best.
- Hold him to a high standard. At the same time, don't let your husband slide with anything less than excellence. We all can become complacent, and it is very helpful to have others remind us to live up to our own standards. Help your spouse be his best.
- Be thankful. Appreciate how lucky you are to have found a caring, responsible, stable, good, Godly man in this world, and let him know that you know it.
- Demand respect. You cannot keep respect unless you insist upon it. There is no excuse for a man disrespecting his wife, but some do. Demand and command respect at all times.

Fathers, Let Them Go

SACRED STONE #56

You cannot serve your little girl by being overprotective.

No one is more overprotective than a doting father is of his daughter. Let's face it, it's easier for a father to let his son go into the world, because we're taught that boys thrive on challenge. But girls? We want to shelter them, protect them, turn them into princesses and lock them in a tower. Dads, all locking your daughters in a tower does is make it impossible for a prince to find them. You cannot serve your little girl by being overprotective.

SACRED STONE #57

Parents must rear their daughters to be strong, forthright, intelligent women who understand who they are and who they must become in order to serve God's family design.

Girls seem more vulnerable than boys. They're physically weaker and sexually more vulnerable. But if you have taught them well, they are also empathic and intuitive and understand how to use the power they possess. Give them street smarts and practical savvy, remind them you love them and let them go. No worthy man ever marries a princess, because he knows he will be second-best in his own household. Rather than create a princess, create a strong, forthright, intelligent woman who understands who she is and who she must become in order to serve God's family design.

6

Character, Respect & Discipline

"Each of you must respect his mother and father, and you must observe my Sabbaths."

—Leviticus 19:3

SACRED STONE #58

When you build a family with a strong sense of character, a culture of respect and strong discipline, you don't have to worry about keeping up a façade.

Too many of us put all our effort into keeping up the façade of the perfect family. We think if our children are always well-dressed and perfectly behaved, and we drive around in a fancy car and live in a big house, we will have the perfect family. But family is about character, respect and discipline. It is about following rules, doing what is right and treating every member of the family as a worthwhile person. When you build a family with a strong sense of character, a culture of respect and strong discipline, you don't have to worry about keeping up the façade. Your family's character will shine through on its own. That is what people will see, and what they will truly admire.

We have spoken a great deal in this book about the dangers that face young people today—drugs, pregnancy, gangs and so on. Those are all legitimate. However, the best way to ensure that your children do not end up wasting their lives in some criminal pursuit or an illegitimate household is to help them develop the character, respect and discipline to make the right choices. When these three essentials are the foundation of your family—along with love and worship of God—you won't have to worry. You can let your children go into the world with confidence, knowing they will be all right.

But how do you build character, respect and discipline into the very fabric of your family? That is what this chapter is all about.

SACRED STONE #59
If you don't have respect in your family, create it.

Just as Jesus is the head of the Church, the father is the head of the home. The man who is head of his household has made that transition into fatherhood and earned the trust, confidence and respect of his wife and, especially, of his children. He has reached this position not based on what he says, but on what he does. Talk is cheap. Acting based on principles, strong personal morals and the dictates of God is the only way to gain lasting respect from your family members. In other words:

A man can only command the degree of respect that he earns.

A man can only take his family to the level that he himself has achieved. If you disrespect yourself by striving for anything less than greatness, you cannot expect your family to respect you. A man needs to excel in his own life to serve as an example of excellence and to pull his family along with him into a better future.

In order to earn the respect as the manager of the family, you must act in a managerial manner. You must make sure the systems of the family are being upheld and running properly. You must take responsibility for bringing in the money to support your family, paying the bills on time, and handling conflict and challenges.

If your family does not respect you because you have not earned their respect, it is time to make an effort to change. You can't just decide tomorrow that your family is going to start respecting you if you don't change the things you have been doing. Insanity is doing the same thing over and over and expecting different results!

Major change does not come easily; it is a process. You may have to take a hard look at yourself and ask what you have done in the past that has cost you your family's respect, and how you could have made different decisions. Then, alter those behaviors in the future. This is not easy; it requires a certain degree of humility to examine one's failings in the past and acknowledge them. But without this kind of self-examination, it is extremely difficult to change your behavior and realize that in the past, you have made mistakes that have cost you your family's respect.

Once you understand the missteps of the past, call on the creative nature of God that resides within you and ideas will come. God will show you the path. Once you have envisioned the changes you need to make, the spark of the divine will help you bring them to fruition. You will begin to act differently, with new wisdom, and your actions will spark a new sense of respect and honor within the other members of your family.

Remember, whatever you don't have dominion over has dominion over you. A father must have dominion over his family to earn its respect. A weak man ultimately produces a weak family. This has a "domino effect" in that a weak family produces a weak church, which then produces a weak community, which ultimately produces a weak nation. Your success in molding your family according to the commandments of God has a wider-ranging effect than you ever thought possible.

SACRED STONE #60
You cannot have authority without fear.

Most of us have a very healthy respect for the laws of society. We don't rob banks because we don't want to go to jail. We don't speed on the highway when we see a police cruiser because we don't want to get a ticket. But if there weren't consequences for those actions, who knows what we would do? We'd probably drive as fast as we wanted. We might even rob a bank or two. But we don't, because we respect the authority of the law and don't want to suffer the penalties. If it's not the law we respect, it's the moral authority behind "Thou shalt not steal" and God's other commandments.

The same is true with raising children. All children need mentors, and sometimes, children need to have a healthy fear of their mentors if those mentors are to be effective. This is not brutality, but honesty. We are motivated in some way by fear in every aspect of our lives: fear of social embarrassment, fear of our health deteriorating if we do not take care of it, fear of firing and bankruptcy and homelessness if we do not perform well at our jobs. Fear is a part of human life, and the astute parent understands how to create and use this powerful force.

Mentors who ought to be reasonably feared include teachers, coaches, and yes, parents. Teachers and coaches cannot do their jobs unless their students have a healthy fear of the repercussions that will occur if they do not follow the rules set down in the class-room and on the playing field. Look at what happens when you take the consequences away. We've taken corporal punishment out of the schools, and now we have students beating up on teachers. Schools regularly allow "social promotion," in which students who fail their classes are moved ahead with the rest of the class rather than being held back. In theory, this promotes self-esteem. What it really does is teach children that adults have no teeth behind their rules. We've empowered students to be abusive. Children have to know that if they break the rules, there will be punishment, and that punishment *will* be carried out.

It is the same in the home. Rules must be established, and parents must be perceived as having the authority to enforce those rules and deliver the consequences if they are not obeyed. When I was a young child and my father walked in the door, our house went into complete submission. There wasn't a lot of laughing and playing around my father, and when we did get too loud, all my father had to do was give us a look. He rarely even had to speak, and if he did, he would say just one word: "Don't." We understood that just fine. It was the law in our house: When Dad came home, the music was turned down, the TV became much softer, and everything was quiet. We respected the office of fatherhood in part because we were afraid of the consequences of breaking its rules.

Children, obey your parents; this is the right thing to do because God has placed them in authority over you. Honor your father and mother. This is the first of God's Ten Commandments that ends with a promise. And this is the promise: that if you honor your father and mother, yours will be a long life, full of blessing. —(Ephesians 6:1–3)

As parents, you have to make sure your children understand that you are the authority and there *will* be consequences if you are not obeyed. Do not allow other family members step in to bend the rules or soften the penalty. Don't make the mistake of playing "good cop/bad cop" with your kids or letting them pit one parent against the other. Present a united front with a single voice, and you will earn your children's honor. You will raise children who respect authority and live good lives.

SACRED STONE #61

Set boundaries for your children and enforce them.

I cannot stress enough the importance of discipline and putting healthy boundaries in a child's life. It teaches them respect for authority, helps them develop self-discipline, and builds character.

Even a child is known by his actions, by whether his conduct is pure and right. —(Proverbs 20:11)

When my wife and I use to travel with our five children, we insisted that while we were in services preaching, our children had to know how to sit quietly and attentively in the church. If they were allowed to laugh or talk amongst themselves or fall asleep, they would have made a mockery of us not just as parents, but as a church. So we taught them to respect spaces and places in our home as well as outside of it. We taught them to just sit and close their eyes and meditate, sometimes for hours. If they were talking too much in the car, we would tell everybody in the car to activate their own personal "mute" buttons and we would have 30 minutes of silence. It was a wonderful sound!

As a result, long before our children started going to school, they already knew how to sit still and be quiet. They never went running around in other peoples' homes or in restaurants. We never had problems with them screaming or running away when we traveled through the airport or went to the shopping mall, because they knew their boundaries. People would ask us how we got our children to behave, and we'd say, "They're good children, but they also had a lot of work and discipline." We had to hold the line on discipline, because we knew if we didn't, we'd be apologizing to people wherever we went for our children's behavior and it would have been an embarrassment to us. Not only that, but we wouldn't be doing our children any favors by letting them run wild.

Discipline your son and he will give you happiness and peace of mind. —(Proverbs 29:17)

No doubt you have witnessed parents in public who cannot control their children. You'll see a mortified mother whose son is lying on the floor of a public restaurant throwing a kicking, screaming tantrum. Or perhaps it's a teenage girl talking back to her mother in a store in tones that would have gotten me a serious spanking if I'd used them with my father. These are classic examples of parents who have lost control through negligence or weakness. Let's face it, it can be hard to be the "bad guy." But when the situation calls for it, it's important to remind yourself that you're doing what's best for your child. In the long run, they will thank you.

Too many parents excuse bad behavior with sentiments like, "But he's only a child." Every child must be taught limits and boundaries. Otherwise, when that "child" walks into a bank with a gun at age 30, what excuse will you use then?

SACRED STONE #62

God did not intend for one person to raise a child alone.

Community is an extension of the family.

No doubt you've heard the old African proverb, "It takes a village to raise a child." This is why God created families and communities. He did not intend for one person to raise a child alone.

There is an interconnection between us all. Your child's actions affect not only your family, but the entire community. If your child becomes a gateway for drug dealership, this is a problem for the whole community. Your community is meant to be an extension of your family. When people in your community see a child in danger, they should care for that child as if he is their own. In the same way, when they see him doing wrong, they should discipline him as their own. Each adult in the community has not only the right but the responsibility to hold a child accountable for his or her actions. That was how it was done when I was growing up.

Unfortunately, there has been hesitancy in recent years to embrace the collective responsibility for our children, and this has produced an abominable deterioration of authority in our midst. A couple of years ago we told parents that if their children were in Children's Church and they misbehaved, they would be disciplined. Well, some parents took their children out. They said, "You're not gonna discipline my baby." Friends, if we cannot entrust our children to one other in the Kingdom, what example are we giving to the world? Parents must understand that community discipline is not an act of power but of love—a lesson given in love to a child who must learn that the ways in which God has ordered his Kingdom are not subject to the child's whim.

There is a need for the united brandishing of strength and effort to restore order in our communities. Your child should become our child. Every woman should be every child's mother, and every man should be every child's father. Grandmothers, grandfathers, aunts, uncles and good neighbors should all be welcomed into a "parenting squad" that takes responsibility for the actions of every child within its circle of influence. That's the duty of every adult. Political correctness and so-called "progressive parenting" do not enter into the discussion. Old-fashioned love, authority and respect have proven for centuries to be the best ways to get children to behave.

SACRED STONE #63

Success is passed down through behavior.

You are your habits. Habits become behaviors and behaviors become your life. Poverty is a behavior and prosperity is a behavior. Why does a rich kid become a rich adult? Because he has been trained by his mother and father to have certain habits that support becoming rich. No doubt, the wealthy parents had certain routines that they followed during the week, and they demanded that their children follow them as well.

You have to do the same with your children. You must put them on track to arrive at the destination of success. Someone asked me once, "What do you do if your children don't want to go to church?" I replied, "My kids grew up with me going to church. That is what we do. They don't know any other way. Not going to church is not an option for them." Church is not a choice. It is part of the fabric of our lives. My children wouldn't dream of not going to church any more than they would dream of not breathing.

Sometimes another kid would come around and say, "Hey, come hang out on the street with us instead." My kids would come back to me and complain that their friend's father lets him hang out and play games instead of going to church. And I'd just tell them, "That father is grooming his child for one thing, we're grooming you for something else." And that would be the end of the discussion. No pleading. No disobeying. Just acceptance. Part of the reason my children took such authority so well was that they knew I truly was grooming them for something great, because I lived the example of what I had in mind for them. They saw what I had become and knew they were on the way to doing the same.

You have to set examples for your kids and be a role model. If you live a life that is unholy before your children, I guarantee they will model your behavior. They don't know any better! You are their first mentor. Your every action will produce a reaction, and no matter how much you beg and plead with your children to do as you say, they will do as you do.

The flip side of this is to not pass down behaviors that make no sense to you just because that's how "it's always been done." When I was growing up, every time my mother cooked a ham for dinner she cut both ends off the ham. I asked her why she did that and she said her mother did it that way and so did her grandmother. For generations, women in our family cut both ends off the ham before they cooked it. We finally found out that it started because my great-grandma's pan was too small to hold the whole ham. She cut both ends off to make it fit into the pan. For years we'd been throwing away perfectly good meat because it was always done that way.

If a behavior doesn't make sense to you, don't just pass it on. Ask questions before you model it for your children. Only model those behaviors that lead to success.

SACRED STONE #64

Help children learn the right ways
to deal with life's challenges.

Life ain't simple. As adults, we know that. But our children don't, and before we release them into the world, we have to teach them how to deal with the challenges life's guaranteed to throw at them. We have to help them understand that life isn't always fair. Bad things can happen to good people (and vice versa). We need to help them learn how to deal with feelings like anger, sadness, frustration and disappointment. We have to show them how to love. And the earlier we start teaching them these things, the better.

But wait a minute, you're saying. How can my little boy or little girl grasp concepts like this when they're so young? I've got one simple tool for you to use with very young children: *fairy tales*.

When you read fairy tales to your children, you help them feel protected and safe, because the bad guy always gets it in the end. This is especially important for our kids who feel alone, out of place, or like outcasts. In Star Wars, the Lord of the Rings and Harry Potter, there is always someone who is an outcast, and there is always a wise wizard or a magical princess to love that child regardless of who he is, and help him come out a winner. Our children learn that there is always someone to help them, and this develops the subconscious part of them that needs to feel safe.

Another thing about fairy tales—the good guy wins in the end because he (or she) has strong character and qualities that help him become a better, stronger human being in the eyes of God. Children see that qualities like honesty, perseverance, kindness, and compassion help them win in the end. They learn they have to confront challenges and overcome them—to slay the dragons that they will encounter in life instead of running and hiding from them.

Fairy tales help children understand what they're going though and reassure them that they have the skills and character to face the Big Bad Wolf and get through it. They also provide role models and heroes for children to emulate. Every child needs a hero!

As our children get older, they will already understand that every time they have the opportunity to confront the "dragons" in life, they have the opportunity to grow. Look at the Bible. The enemy started out as serpent in Genesis and became a dragon in Revelation. When you come to new levels, you meet new devils. Raising our children to be confident human beings with strong characters will help them overcome the devil every time.

Jesus went through hell for us. We have to teach our kids that when they're going through hell, they need to just keep on pedaling! Fairy tales, family support and lots of love teach them that even though bad things can happen, the great majority of the time if they face those things with courage, determination and hope, they will get through them and come to victory. One of the most vital lessons you can teach your child (some adults need to learn this as well):

SACRED STONE #65

It's not what happens to you, but how you respond to it that determines how you live.

Bad things do happen. People get sick. Nice people become victims of crime. Hurricane Katrinas can overturn everything in life you thought was secure. But when difficult times come, you have two choices. You can react with anger or fear—cursing God or hiding in a corner. Or you can respond with determination—come out fighting, committed to doing whatever it takes to regain your equilibrium and rebuild your life. More often than not, determination, hope and faith are all-powerful. Passing on this lesson is one of the most important gifts you can give to your children.

What if, after all your efforts at raising your children with God and building a strong, solid family, your family starts to have problems? Don't feel bad. Every family has challenges. Your job is to identify and overcome those challenges.

A dysfunctional family is like a body that has a bone out of joint. It throws the whole being out of balance. A dislocated bone causes pain in the entire body, and a dislocation of the family system causes emotional pain for everyone. At the same time, the fact of a bone being out of joint is surreal and frightening, making everyone in the family feel as if the normal world has vanished. It's a difficult time, but you can bring your family through it.

SACRED STONE #66

A dysfunctional family is like a body that has a bone out of joint.

The first step is to locate that bone. Look for the problem in the family. Is a child bringing home bad grades? Spending too much time playing violent video games? Hanging out with the wrong crowd? Is the father drinking too much or shutting out the family instead of spending time with them? Is the mother depressed? These are just a few of the symptoms of a dysfunctional family.

Next, you have to fix the bone. Sometimes the bone must be broken in order to stimulate healing. This is the hard part. Since the pain of breaking the bone can be more intense than living with the pain of the dislocation, it may be easier just to live with it than to make the effort (and go through the pain) of changing it. But that is the only way to fix it.

If your family is dysfunctional, find the bone and fix it. This may mean you have to "break" the way you have been living and get it back on the right track. You must endure a little pain to prevent a lifetime of it. It is the breaking that stimulates healing and growth. Change can be frightening and difficult to stick with, even when you know it is the right thing for everyone. If sensible change were easy, more people would quit smoking! But it's usually hard. When the time comes that you know you must change the way your family has been living—break the bone and let it mend—then focus on three critical steps:

1. Ask God's guidance. Spend time in prayer or meditation and get in touch with the divine in you. You will find God's wisdom inside you and that will help you choose the right path.

2. Communicate with your family. Talk with everyone sincerely and honestly about the problems you see and the need for changes. There may be disagreement. Hear it but do not waver. Be firm and insist that changes will happen.

3. Be consistent. Once the changes are in place, you must not let your family go backward. That's like getting your leg out of a cast, then over-exerting yourself so that you re-injure it. Make sure everyone knows the rules and follows them, and follow them yourself.

Families can and do heal. Doing so can often bring you and yours closer than you have ever been before.

7

God in Your Home

But you, dear friends, build yourselves up in your most holy faith and pray in the Holy Spirit.

—Jude 1:20

When you praise, you raise stronger families. A father's home is his altar. When a father takes the time to weigh his responsibilities in prayer, he becomes a man of solutions. God will give him a ready answer for every challenge his family faces and lead them into a deeper knowledge of the Lord. Praise will help a family through a challenging time. Praise will raise you up!

So the house of the father is also the House of the Father. In older language, "house" meant not only the building in which a family lived, but the family line itself, from generation to generation. When the British press talks about the House of Windsor, that's what they mean: the line of generations. So the place your family resides is also where God finds your part of His extended family. God always has a place in the home, just as He always has a place at the heart of every family... whether that family knows it or not!

SACRED STONE #67
Children learn about God through their view of their parents.

Mothers and fathers impart the values and righteous standards of the Bible to their children by modeling those patterns right before their eyes. It is the role of the parents to reflect and engrave God's personality upon their children. The actions you and your spouse take as parents every day will show your children how the will of God is to be carried out in the world. Your actions must match your words, or you will appear hypocritical. And hypocrisy is the fastest way to lose your children's respect.

Why must parents engrave God's personality? In the eyes of your children, your face is the first face of God they meet. Your children form their first impressions about God through their impressions of you. Wow. That's powerful. You are God's proxy on this earth—you are literally God pressed out into this material reality—and so each act, word and touch a mother or father makes is also a touch from God. What you say and do will tell your children more about the nature of God than anything they read in the Bible or hear in church.

Part of Your Promise to God

SACRED STONE #68

Parents must understand that they do not possess their children for their own purposes, but their children shall be arrows shot from their quiver to carry on the work of the Lord.

God has given you the seed and made it fertile; now you must keep your promise to God by raising your children to follow the path of the Lord. This covenant must exist in a parental relationship, and you may not enter into it lightly. However you present yourself to your children will be a revelation of your God to them. This is one of the most important reasons why men and women must not enter into a marriage or parenthood until they are mature enough to handle the responsibilities. You must be able to fulfill your responsibility to God.

As parents, you must understand that you do not possess your children for your own purposes, but that they shall be arrows shot from your quiver to carry on the work of the Lord. Your children are your love and your life and the center of your everyday activity, but they are intended to carry the will of God forward in time after you are gone. Once the Lord has called you home, your children will carry on His work, and then their children will do the same, unto the end of the world.

Your ultimate charge as parents is to carry out God's will embodied in your children by teaching them in the ways of God and guiding them in the ways to live well and live according to God's economy. That is why God gave you the means to have children: children grow into adults who, if raised in God's ways and wisdom, become His hands in shaping the world.

Teaching Children What God Is

SACRED STONE #69

Over a period of years, you must educate your children in the nature of God.

The most elemental question children will ask their parents when they come into some form of spiritual awareness is, "What is God?" The concept of God is overfilled with misconceptions, bad theology and outright delusions. In their early lives, children will be told that God is:

- An old man with a white beard on a throne
- A figment of the imagination
- Vengeful and angry

- Capricious and apt to bring misfortune on someone for no reason
- A "cosmic consciousness" with no form
- A female

When your children are old enough to begin asking questions about the nature of God, they are old enough to begin hearing the answers. Over a period of years, you must educate them in the nature of God. God is none of the above: He is the Universe, the Father of Jesus Christ, and the Creator of our material reality. God is Spirit, that which is without physical form and physical expression. Most vital, God is us. We are expressions of the Almighty pressed into this material consciousness as our wonderfully complex brains and bodies, created by God so that He would have a physical agent to work His will on the material plane, where as Spirit He does not reside. God needs us to affect the material realm and fulfill His plan for it!

We serve the Divine and we are of the Divine. Most of us never realize our connection to the divinity within us, but it is our responsibility as parents to guide our children along the path to understanding God's nature so they may make the effort to reach the divine part of themselves.

These are the basic points every parent should share with their children in response to the question, "What is God?":

- God is good.
- God is the Father of the Universe.
- God is love.
- God is Spirit, not flesh.
- God is the Father of Jesus Christ.
- God is in you and each of us.
- God speaks to us when our minds are quiet and at peace.
- God has a system by which His world works, just as our family has a system that keeps things harmonious.

- God has a purpose for each of us.
- God wants you to discover God in you and reach your highest potential.

SACRED STONE #70

Teach children to turn to God in their hour of need.

What do you turn to in your hour of calamity? That is a revelation of who your God is. If you show your children that the way to handle conflict and disappointment is by drinking alcohol, smoking marijuana or snorting cocaine, they will believe that they should turn to some substance outside of themselves to handle their own problems, too. But if you turn to God and ask for His help and guidance, you will teach your children to turn to Him as well.

God is our refuge and strength, a very present help in trouble. —(Psalms 46:1)

When you let your body and spirit become altered by substances, those substances take dominion over you. Whatever you don't have dominion over takes dominion over you and reduces you from the image that God has created for you. Let God take dominion in your hour of need. This is the example you should set for your children.

When you fight and war among yourselves in the face of adversity, you teach your children the lesson that despair is the right response to the travails of life. Understand, God does not reach into our lives and control everything that happens. If He did, we would be puppets. People who believe that are simply too infantile or frightened to live without some kind of guarantee that everything will be all right. But bad things happen. Mistakes get made. But God never sends us more than we can handle. When you understand this, the troubled times of your life will build your character and make you stronger. This is why it is so critical that you teach your kids to turn to God when things get tough, because God will show them the way to use life's hardships to create a brighter future. If instead they turn to substances, anger, violence, crime or simply give up, then they squander their potential.

SACRED STONE #71
You must make time for God in your home.

Life gets busy, as you know, and few things are busier than a family with multiple school-age kids. There's work, classes, homework, practice, meals, extracurricular activities and on and on. It can be challenging to find time to sit down and have a meal together. But it's important that amidst all the running around, you make time for your family to have an audience with God.

One of the best times for this is the family dinner. This is a declining tradition in America, as more families split off to do their own things. I think this is a huge error, as there is no better time for parents and children to communicate and to share time with the Lord than at the dinner table. Just the act of saying grace alone invokes the presence of the Lord and blesses the meal. From there, talk to your children about their day and ask them to share with you what each event tells them about the journey God is sending them on. You'll be surprised how quickly even the busiest families become hooked on this healthy, peace-giving ritual.

It is also important to set aside an expanse of time a few times a week to talk about God and spirituality. This could be an evening Bible study, group prayer or meditation, or even just a quiet, undisturbed family conversation about the Lord, faith, and the church, with no questions off limits. No cell phones, no video games, no distractions.

Finally, make sure each child learns at an early age to pray or meditate on his or her own each night before going to bed. This can be as simple as saying a traditional prayer thanking God for the day or as complex as a meditation rite in which the person calms his or her mind in order to hear the voice of God clearly. Let each child chose his or her own path. Just make sure that such time is a part of the bedtime ritual from very early on, so by the time kids are in school, prayer and meditation are parts of their daily lives.

SACRED STONE #72

You must make a place for God in your home.

God is everywhere, but He still needs a dedicated place in your home. This is because we are material beings as well as beings of spirit, and it is useful for us to have a physical place that we can think of as the place where we turn our minds and spirits to the divine.

I don't mean you should build a shrine to the Lord like Buddhists do, but instead consecrate a place in your home—even your backyard—to God and keep it holy. What does this mean? That when you are in this place as a family, you will turn your minds toward the spiritual. This must become a place for contemplation, prayer, discussion of the manifestations of God in your lives, or simple silence and quieting of mind. When a single person is in this space with the intent of using it as a place of prayer or meditation, the rest of the family must respect it.

So as you can see, creating a place for God is really about having a space where your mind is on God and only God. This is a fantastic way to carve out time and awareness of the need for family spiritual time in the midst of the craziness of day to day life.

Church: It's Not Just for Sundays Anymore

SACRED STONE #73

Learning that church is the heart of the week's life is a vital lesson for children.

In my family, church wasn't a chore. It wasn't an option. It wasn't even a question. It was just what we did on Sunday. It was as natural as breathing: get up, clean up, have breakfast, get dressed in fine clothes, go to church and spend three or four hours with our faith community. That was what we did. Some folks watch football every Sunday. We went to church. That's how I've raised my children.

Children will not always want to go to church. They will want to sleep in, to play games, to watch sports or cartoons, to do anything but get cleaned up and sit in a big open space where they have to remain still and quiet. But as we discussed before, this is part of their discipline. More than that, learning that church is the heart of the week's life is a vital lesson for children. In your family, your offspring must come to appreciate that church is something without which the family cannot function. It really is as simple as that.

You see, the church is a community of hundreds or thousands of individuals, each of them a face of God in this world. That community sticks together; when someone is sick, the church community comes together with food, love and support. When someone is lost or hurt, people jump to help. When someone is having a spiritual crisis, the church family (an extension of your own family) helps guide them through to the light with the wisdom of the elders. The individual family cannot thrive and survive without the love, support, assistance and collected wisdom of the men and women who make up the church community. None of us succeeds alone; none of us knows all the ways of God. We need each other.

Children need to understand the codes of conduct regarding the church:

- They must always dress cleanly and in their best clothes
- They must be quiet and listen
- They must always respect elders
- They must thank everyone who does even the smallest kindness
- They must return that kindness to someone else in the church
- They must take that church spirit into the rest of their lives

That last point leads me into the next lesson. You must also teach your children that the church does not end at the walls of a building, nor do its services only occur on Sundays. The entire world is God's church, and services never cease. Every day and every person is a potential member of your church family. By training your youngsters to embody the kindness, faith, compassion, strength and awareness that they find in church each day, when they head into the world you will extend God's family and do your church honor. You will be doing God's work.

I am not suggesting that you teach your children to proselytize. I am saying that you should teach them to passionately *embody* the teachings of the church and the will of God in everything they do. They should treat every day as Sunday and every action of their minds and bodies as testimony of the greatness of the Divine. Actions speak far louder than words, so when your children take church with them into the wider world, they will expand God's family and your church community. And for that, you can take justified pride.

SACRED STONE #74

You must teach your children to pray.

Children naturally talk to God. Once they learn that there is Someone there to speak to, they will speak to Him. But they do not understand how to pray in the sense that someone who understands the How and Why of God understands prayer. That you must teach them.

Early on, it's fine to let children pray to God in their own childish way. They need to learn to get comfortable with the words and the idea of talking to the Creator. But when they get into school, talk to them by saying you think they're "big enough" now to begin talking to God in a different way. Then explain that God talks as much as He listens, and for them to hear what he is saying, they need to quiet their minds and speak from the inside.

This is when it's useful to help your child create a bedtime ritual so he or she can get in the mindset to have a dialogue with God. Light, music or a certain set of activities can contribute to a peaceful, quiet mind. Then you can work with your child to pray and quiet the stream of thoughts that run through all our minds, getting to a state of stillness where we can hear the "still, small voice" that speaks to us all the time. Only when we are in a state of peace and solitude can we hear what God is saying.

God in Your Marriage

SACRED STONE #75

In a marriage, the husband and wife must agree to turn to God for counsel and guidance.

We've been talking all this time about God in the family as it relates to your children, but what about your marriage? Every mature, loving, mutually respectful marriage is blessed by God, but what is the role of God in your marriage? Should you listen to God or your husband or wife?

My answer: listen to both. God is not a marriage counselor. Maintaining your marriage is your job. You are responsible for establishing the system under which your marriage will thrive, and for keeping communication open between you and your spouse. Beyond that, you must agree when to turn to God for counsel and guidance.

God does not take sides. That is not His role. God is your source of wisdom and strength and love in a marriage. When you feel yourself losing patience with your wife and suddenly you realize that you must say, "I love you" and everything will be OK, that is God working through you. When you cannot get through to your husband, and without warning the right words suddenly appear in your mouth, that is God. You must invite God into your marriage, so that neither of you is playing God off the other.

SACRED STONE #76

Your marriage is a promise to the Lord.

When you arrive at a place where you are ready to embark on a mature marriage, consecrate your marriage to God. Tell Him that though you both accept responsibility for your relationship and family, you invite God in and ultimately bow to His will regarding your marriage. What He reveals to you, you will obey. When He advises you, you will listen.

Your marriage is a promise to the Lord. Speak that promise to each other and welcome God into your marriage as counselor, friend, guide and father, and you will have a blessed union no matter what life sends your way. Amen.

8

The Spousal Bond

The husband should give to his wife her conjugal rights, and likewise the wife to her husband. For the wife does not have authority over her own body, but the husband does; likewise the husband does not have authority over his own body, but the wife does. Do not deprive one another except perhaps by agreement for a set time, to devote yourselves to prayer, and then come together again, so that Satan may not tempt you because of your lack of self-control.

—1 Corinthians 7:3–5

SACRED STONE #77

When a marriage is in trouble, the family is in trouble.

It is true that the gift of children from God strengthens a marriage and deepens the bond between husband and wife. But too often parents focus so much attention on the children that they lose sight of their own relationship. When a husband and wife start to take each other for granted, or stop appreciating the very qualities that brought them together in the first place, the marriage is in trouble. And when the marriage is in trouble, the family is in trouble. Strong families are built on strong marriages. Weak marriages produce weak families.

Remember, the most important relationship in the family will always be the relationship between husband and wife. Mothers often lose themselves in their children and forget that they are also wives; husbands can lose themselves likewise in their work, in building something. But at the heart of every stable family is a strong bond between spouses. When it comes time to choose between stabilizing your relationship with your mate or caring for your children's needs, you should always take care of your mate first, because without a strong, solid marriage there is nothing at the heart of the family and it crumbles.

That is why children have no business sticking their noses into the affairs of their parents. When they argued or got angry or upset, I asked my parents what was wrong; all children do. They told me not to worry about it. It was none of my business, even if I could have understood it. Children have no place in the affairs of adults. When you and your spouse fight over money, sex, infidelity or anything else, put on a brave face for your kids but inform them in no uncertain terms to keep their eyes and ears to themselves. Adults must sort out adult work. You must establish the boundaries of privacy or you will not be able to solve your troubles without them affecting your kids.

SACRED STONE #78

Continue to be husband and wife, not just mother and father.

At the core of the above message is this simple truth: you must always be husband and wife first, before you are mother and father, mentor and teacher, host and hostess, church father and church mother. Your relationship must *always* be first. It is important to make a conscious effort to regain some of the aspects of your relationship that you had before you had children.

This is not easy. Becoming a parent changes your life completely; don't believe anyone who tells you otherwise. Your time is committed to those small people who run around in all directions and need you to help them do everything. But that's all the more reason to pray, gain wisdom from God, and work with your mate to carve out some "pre-parenting" space in your lives that can bring back some of what you had before you became mother and father. That's the best way to keep your marriage sparkling and alive. Some of what I'm talking about:

- **Sex.** A couple needs to have sex often. If they do not, they are opening up a wedge in the bedchamber. Having sex often may not be easy when there is an infant crying for a bottle in the middle of the night and both parents are dealing with too much stress and not enough sleep. *But if your spouse wants to have sex, do not refuse.* It doesn't matter if you are tired or have a headache or need to prepare for that big meeting at work tomorrow. Part of the covenant of marriage under God is that your body is no longer yours. Once you say, "I do," your body has become your spouse's body and his or her body has become yours. Sex is your sacred time for you and your partner to commune, share your spirits and be together as one. Never let your sex life fade or you doom your marriage.

- **Time.** The greatest casualty of the marriage with children is time the husband and wife have to spend with each other. As with other aspects of your marriage, you must work to recapture some of that personal time. So sit down and schedule time to spend with each other when your children are not around. This could be after they have gone to bed, early in the morning when they have not awoken yet, or even a designated time on a set night of the week when the kids know not to bother you unless the house is burning down. Set aside a private space where you and your spouse can spend this time. It doesn't have to be about sex; you can talk, read together, pray together or just *be*. Or talk to your church community and find a reliable babysitter, then get out one Saturday night a month.

- **Passion.** This doesn't necessarily mean sex, but instead a passion to be with each other. Remember when you first were dating and you could talk on the phone for hours? The other person sparked that kind of excitement in you. Take the time to rediscover that passion for being together, engaging in each other's interests, listening as well as talking, and learning new things about your spouse. You should constantly be surprising one another your whole lives.

- **Privacy.** Private time? With children? You're kidding, right? No. It's vital that you have a place in your home where you and your spouse can have privacy. In all likelihood, this will be your bedchamber. Make sure it has a lock on the door, and make sure your children know that when you are inside with the door locked, you are not to be disturbed unless there is an emergency. Privacy is a precious thing for parents; gift some to yourselves.

- **Money.** There is another reason to make sure you continue to have sex with each other: money. Money flows better when love is being made in the bedroom. Couples who have a lot of sex are prosperous; couples who have no or little sex are not because there's no exchange of goods. If you can't close the deal in the bedroom, you can't close it in the boardroom, or at the mortgage company, or wherever. Sex keeps the good energy flowing in the marriage, and that energy is passed on to the children, so they feel the good energy in their home.

SACRED STONE #79

All marriages will experience hard times.

We humans are funny. We convince ourselves that life will always be smooth sailing and that difficult times will never come to us, or if they do we will always be able to see them coming. Nonsense. It is one thing to be optimistic about your marriage; it is another to be complacent. When complacency sets in, neglect follows. That's when you stop doing the work that keeps a marriage vital and decay sets in. When that disease takes hold, it's often too late to save the patient. The marriage dies and the family is broken apart.

Instead, expect hard times in your marriage. Do not assume that all will always be well, you'll always feel passionate love for your partner, and you will always agree. Instead, assume that you will disagree, know that there will be times you wish you were not married, and understand that love is a *decision*, not an emotion. You decide every day to love your husband or wife; it is a conscious effort on your part. You cannot take it for granted, or you will lose the ability to make the effort, like an athlete who lets a muscle atrophy.

Hard times are nothing to be ashamed of; they occur in every marriage. But if you do not develop the skills to deal with them, you will ignore the warning signs until it's too late. Do you think it's possible to be with someone for 30, 40 or 50 years and not experience disease, accident, mistrustful acts, intense arguments or other crises? Of course not. In the course of time, things happen. Sometimes they occur for no apparent reason. But if you condition yourself to be prepared for the hard times in your marriage, you will not be shocked when they arrive, and you will come out of them stronger.

See the Soul, Not Only the Body

SACRED STONE #80

In your marriage, you must train yourself to look beyond the flesh and see the person, the walking spirit created by God who you married. That is the person who will transcend time.

Because we are material, physical beings in this reality, we tend to focus on the physical rather than the underlying spirit of a person. That is understandable; we give our attention to what is before our eyes. But in your marriage, you need to train yourself to look beyond the flesh and see the person, the walking spirit created by God who you married. That is the person who will transcend time.

The reason is simple: humans age. Our flesh grows old and changes. The tight body of youth gives way to the mottled, not-so-tight body of middle age and beyond. If you focus your attention only on the fleshly, outer aspect of your spouse, then you will certainly lose attraction for that person over time. You will find yourself drawn to younger men or women who spark your sexual drive. You will become dissatisfied in your marriage and risk an act of infidelity that could destroy it.

Instead, teach yourself to always look beyond the physical to the spirit and soul of the man or woman with whom you fell in love. The body changes, but the soul does not. It is eternal. The kindness, passion, creativity, humor, love, intelligence and honesty of your partner will not lessen from age 20 to age 80; in fact, it will often grow greater. And as the flesh ages, the spirit provides compensations: greater comfort with one another, greater knowledge of each other's sexuality, deeper shared experience. Remember why you fell in love in the first place. It wasn't just a nice rear end.

Grow From Your Spouse's Strength

I am continually astonished at the areas in which I am weak that my wife is strong. It humbles me to be around a person who is so powerful when I am so at sea. And yet, there are areas in which I can't be matched that she is weak. That is what a mature, complementary relationship is about. You and your mate should make each other stronger.

Imagine that you and your spouse married at age 25. If you both live to 85, that's 60 years of marriage! Sixty glorious years of being together almost every day. Learn something from that lifetime association! It is almost certain that your wife or husband will be gifted in ways you are not. One of the reasons God created the idea of marriage was so that men and woman could teach each other—so they could each make the other wiser, greater and more able to create positive change in the world. You and your spouse should always be observing how the other handles the situations of life and applying the underlying lessons to your own behavior. In this way, you become more than the sum of your individual spirits. You become greater creatures of God!

A wife who is nervous and tends to worry about everything can learn from a husband who remains calm in the face of uncertainty, that the worst rarely happens, and it's pointless to worry. Worry is a useless emotion. A husband who is impatient with his children and other people can learn from a patient wife that things will come when they will, and acting impatient only makes them take longer. You and your spouse have much to teach each other by word and example. You have only to open your eyes and your heart and learn.

SACRED STONE #81

Unfaithfulness teaches children distrust and suspicion.

When a spouse is refused sex, he or she will go out wandering and looking for the other woman or other man. As soon as one spouse is unfaithful, the sacredness of the family has been violated. Infidelity is the worst sin a mate can commit against his or her partner, because it violates the trust of the family and shatters the family covenant with God. Families affected by infidelity are rarely ever whole again.

Whenever a spouse cheats, the other spouse knows it on some level. Often they know the exact day it happened—they describe a sensation of just feeling violated. Then, they become the in-house lawyer, asking questions about everything the cheating spouse is doing. Where did you go for lunch? Who did you go with? What did you talk about? What time did you leave work? Why did it take you so long to get home? This creates an atmosphere of tension, anger and resentment that affects the children as well.

Now you have a relationship based on distrust. And just as your children sensed the good energy in your marriage before it got all messed up, now they sense the distrust and suspicion. Unfaithfulness teaches children to be distrustful. It teaches children that they can't put their faith in anyone because that person might not be telling them the truth even after they vowed to do so. In order to fix the damage you've done to the children and make the marriage work again, you have to build that trust back up, and that can be a very hard thing to do. In many cases, it is impossible. Such marriages end in divorce, families are split apart, and years can be required to rebuild any semblance of stability for the children. That's why the children of divorce often end up in unhealthy marriages themselves.

Unfaithfulness also affects the financial stability of the family. Wherever you find immorality, there is poverty. They go hand in hand. Paul tells us in the Bible, *"For this is the will of God, your sanctification: that you should abstain from sexual immorality."* —*(1 Thes. 4:3)* You must remain faithful to the family. To do otherwise is to violate your covenant with God, damage your children and hinder your financial security.

SACRED STONE #82

Give more than expected.

Whenever you are in a partnership, whether it is a business deal, a marriage, or a basketball match, you and your partner have to be equally committed to putting forth your best effort. When one partner gives more than the other, you've got problems. The partner putting in the greater effort starts to feel unappreciated. Eventually, he or she may begin to resent the other person who isn't holding up their end of the deal.

One of the secrets to a strong, successful marriage is to always give more than what is expected of you. Once a man becomes a husband and a woman becomes a wife, they are meant to support and give to each other. When children enter the picture, it can be a challenge to maintain that commitment to your spouse because the children have needs and demands of their own. Mothers, you have to get up and get the kids breakfast and send them off to school even when you have the flu. Fathers, you have to play with the kids and get them out of your wife's hair even though you're tired from work. You both have to make an extra effort to do more than is expected of you. And when your spouse does more than is expected of him or her, acknowledge that effort. Raising a family isn't easy. Appreciation and gratitude go a long way to strengthening the bonds of marriage.

The same principle applies to your children. Don't just show up at their baseball game. Get there a little early, chat with the coach, encourage the team, let your children know you're proud of them. Don't just drop them off at school—volunteer to help out in the classroom or chaperone the field trip. Go the extra mile.

SACRED STONE #83

Give respect and be worthy of it.

Respect is another fundamental part of a healthy marriage. You must both give it and receive it for your relationship to be positive and affirming. A marriage in which one spouse does not respect the other is headed for infidelity and harm; the spouse who does not respect his or her partner will feel free to do anything he or she likes. Respect is essential for a strong family.

Giving respect is the easier part of this equation. As a mature, experienced person, you are bound to recognize that your spouse is a person of knowledge, wisdom and faith equal to you. You are bound to give your spouse your attention and your empathy, and consider his or her concerns in every decision you make. The worst mistake a husband or wife can make is to *dismiss* his mate. When you do that, you tell the other person that he or she is unimportant, foolish, beneath you. In a relationship where you must be equals, that inequality can be disastrous.

Receiving respect is harder. Respect is not given; it is earned. You must always earn and re-earn your mate's respect. Even if you are the man, anointed as head of the household, you must earn your wife's respect. It is not your birthright. Strength in adversity, wise decision-making, fairness, coolness in times of high emotion, hard work and sacrifice are ways to earn respect within the confines of a marriage. If you act consistently, keep your word and treat your mate with respect, you will earn respect in return. When mutual respect flows between husband and wife, a marriage cannot help but be healthful and blessed.

SACRED STONE #84

Marriage is a matter of trust.

Life is about trust. God is about trust. Just as you trust God to give you wisdom and strength and the anointing of His will, God trusts you to fulfill your promises made to Him and to carry out His will. Every day is an act of trust. So you can imagine that more than any other state of being, trust is the most vital to marriage.

When you marry a man or woman, you make yourself vulnerable. You give that person not only everything you have but everything you are. You put yourself in a position to be hurt emotionally, financially, even physically. That demands trust. That is also why marriage is not the purview of the immature or inexperienced; no one without a mature sense of self can know whether a potential mate can be trusted! Only when you have lived a while, come into your wisdom and learned what you are truly looking for in a spouse can you know if a person exhibits qualities that suggest he or she is trustworthy. Until that time, all relationships are learning experiences—sometimes difficult ones.

Trust is simultaneously steel-strong and fragile. It can be the binding that holds the heavy weight of a family together, and at the same time it can be irrevocably splintered by a single stray hair, a bit of lipstick, or an unwise slap. The trust of years can be destroyed in minutes, turned into self-delusion. Trust is like a delicate rose. That is why it is at the heart of every marriage and each marriage's most prized possession. Once trust is gone, there is no true way to get it back. A wife whose husband has cheated will never truly believe in him again; she will always suspect him even if he is innocent.

Husbands and wives, guard your legacy of trust! Keep communication open and encourage the hard questions. Most important, know what signs tell you that you can or cannot trust a potential mate. Then listen to what those signs are trying to tell you, turn to God for wisdom, and pay attention. You will know who has a right to your sacred trust, and trust will be the bedrock upon which you will build your thriving family.

9

Financial Security

"If anyone does not provide for his relatives, and especially for his immediate family, he has denied the faith and is worse than an unbeliever."

—1 Timothy 5:8

SACRED STONE #85

As you grow your family, learn to take joy and contentment and appreciation from those things in life that are not based on consumer purchases.

Money magnifies the good in a family. Money is a multiplier and an enhancer. It gives you the freedom, physically and emotionally, to get the most that you can from your time on Earth. More important than that, it gives you the power to carry out God's will in this reality. Money is a creative force that multiplies the ability of you and your family to do more and become more. And every person on this planet is in a constant state of becoming.

Debt does exactly the opposite. Debt puts a stranglehold around the family's neck. Debt is an all-consuming force of destruction. If a man is impotent, he cannot produce a family. If the head of the family is financially impotent, he cannot produce a secure, strong family. The family cannot realize its dreams and desires. Do whatever you can to avoid debt, but the most time-proven debt avoidance strategy is the one that's often the hardest: self-control.

As you grow your family, learn to take joy and contentment and appreciation from those things in life that are not based on consumer purchases: time with family, music, peaceful mornings, wonderful home-cooked food, time with friends, your garden, time in communion with God. Those things make a man rich yet do not cost him a great deal of wealth. The problem is, we worship Mammon in our society far more than we worship God.

Our consumer culture is all about acquiring things that we do not need in order to feel better about ourselves. Feeling down because you're fat? Buy a $15,000 plasma TV and that will make you feel better! This kind of thinking is a trap. Because eventually the euphoria of a new possession fades and you need to go out and spend more to get that feeling back. Spending is a drug. Debt is an overdose. In his book *Good Debt, Bad Debt*, writer Jon Hanson calls it "debt-abetes."

In this life, you will never gain joy from the things you can buy in a store. Joy comes from other, deeper sources: creating something wonderful, giving to your church, helping others, raising a family, cultivating a group of bosom friends, living simply and appreciating the beauty and wonder of God's world every day. As you make money in life, use it to do those things that bring true joy, such as supporting your church, helping the unfortunate, building a business, or designing a home that fosters a simple, sensually satisfying, healing lifestyle. Only when you stop seeing material things as an end, rather than the means to an end, will you escape the debt disease.

What is Money?

SACRED STONE #86

The purpose of money is within you.

People misquote the Bible all the time when it comes to money. They say, "Money is the root of all evil." Not true. The Bible actually says that the *love* of money is the root of all evil. Money is a tool like any other. As such, it is neutral, neither good nor evil. It is what we do with it. Some use money to fund pornography and start wars and buy drugs. Those are evils. Others use it to start charities and build houses for the poor and grow crops to give us alternative fuels. Those are great goods. The purpose of money is within you.

But what is money? Money is many things—a social contract, a means of exchange—but most of all it is this:

SACRED STONE #87

Money is God's power to create change in the material world.

Interesting way to think about money, isn't it? But what is money but the power to change something? The more money you have, the greater the change you can command. If you have $100, all you can change is the shirt on your back. But what if you have one billion dollars? Then you can change the lives of millions by starting a charity program, buying books for thousands of schools, or creating a business that in turn creates jobs and economic prosperity.

So in gaining more money, you are really gaining the power and authority to transform this world. According to your vision? No, according to God's vision that he shares with you when your mind is quiet. Money grants you the freedom to pursue your ideas, the ability to bring them into material reality, and the influence to grow them to world changing scope. That is how ideas that have transforming mankind, from Habitat for Humanity to Google, have come to fruition. First there is a vision, then someone who understands how to bring that vision to life, then money that moves the people and goods to make that vision appear in our consciousness.

Money is a lot more than what we get in our paychecks.

SACRED STONE #88

If the home is messy, the finances of the family are going to be messy.

Here's one of the laws about money: Money only shows up where order is in place. When your life is messy, your finances will be messy. The two do not seem to be connected, but since money is a reflection of you, how money rests in your life will be a reflection of that life. How you live dictates how you earn.

Fundamentally, money is a concept. It is not the paper or coins we see and hold and carry in our wallets. It is an idea, an agreement that all parties will find this currency of value and accept it for goods and services. But money is also God in the world, and God is a God of order. The act of creation brought order out of chaos. Therefore, money is attracted to order as well. When your home and life are disorderly, money cannot flow into your life as easily, just as water will not flow cleanly down a watercourse that is cluttered and blocked. Money loves order and common sense.

If you want to attract money into your home, make sure your home is in order. I'm not just talking about keeping it clean and tidy, although that is important too. But you also have to make sure your home is in order spiritually and emotionally. If you have not made a place in your home for God, your home is out of order. If your marriage is on the rocks or your children are not respecting their parents—if your family has a bone out of joint—your home is messy. When you clean up your house, the money can come in.

SACRED STONE #89

If your family is spiritually wasteful, money will slip through your fingers.

How do you, your spouse and your children spend your energy and spirit? Is it on helping others, contributing to your church, and giving back to the community? Are you and yours focused on creating a harmonious family life? Or are you spending your energies on conflict, material gain, rivalry and greed? Money reacts to waste by staying away. If you are spiritually wasteful, you will find that opportunities that should come to you go to others.

Think of money as energy. Energy flows to places where the existing energy is coherent and focused. When you are wasting your spirit on unproductive pursuits, money actively bypasses your house and flows where it finds the least resistance. So when your family is in an uproar, you are actively repelling the wealth that could transform your lives! Instead, focus on:

- Maintaining a harmonious household.
- Giving to others.
- Channeling the talents of those in your family in ways that serve God.
- Living simply and peacefully, rather than consuming wildly.
- Conserving your energies for important works and letting others handle the trivial.

What is God's Economy?

God operates in a cosmic economy of His own design. Everything within the earthly realm works within this economy, and nothing gets done without functioning according to the rules of this economic system. The key to God's economy is both simple and eternally complex:

I AM.

I Am is the key to the cosmic economy. What on earth does that mean? It means that to get the things and opportunities you want, you must become them in your mind and spirit. You must act and think as though they are already in manifestation. You see, God does not work in the physical. He is not bound by Time. He is outside of the physical and Time. So rather than manifesting something physical in your life today, He asks you to visualize that thing in your future, to become that thing, which is "I Am." When you do this, God then manifests that thing in your future, assuming you follow through on the actions that you must to bring it into reality—giving, working hard, envisioning the thing already in existence and so on. Then, eventually, your vision becomes reality in your present mind!

God's economy is about mind and spirit, not physical forces. I have benefited from this economy for many years. When I wanted a bigger house, I began to see the house, to thank God for helping me find it, to see myself walking around its rooms. I praised God and lived with that house in my present consciousness, and my consciousness *pulled* that house from my future time stream into my reality! I found the house I had seen in my mind; God brought it to me. And when I found the house, I had also acquired the means to pay for it. I did not have to do anything else, just believe that if I operated according to the Creator's economic system, He would provide.

That is the key. You can manifest wealth, businesses, opportunity and great people in God's system, but only if you unreservedly give yourself to it. God wants you to cast aside caution, live on the edge, and have no other means of support. Then He will shower you with riches. Playing it cautious produces meager, impoverished results. Poor people think poor thoughts! Rich people think big, act boldly and fear nothing! You must state your "I Am" and trust completely in God to send you what you need, without worrying about investors, business plans or anything else. Only when you lean 100% on God will he repay your investment with gold.

So as you go forward from reading this book, ask yourself what you want for your family's future. Is it enough money to live comfortably? Enough to live with total freedom? Enough to start something that will create positive change in the world? Decide what you want for your family's economic tomorrow, then become that thing. Declare "I Am" and have faith in God. What you desire will come to fruition.

SACRED STONE #90

God does not reward waste. Live sensibly.

While you are living your I Am and waiting for your vision to manifest in God's economy, you must simultaneously live in the practical realm of your family's economy. That is, you must pay the bills, try to save money, and work to bring in a decent income. In other words, you must be financially responsible and live within your means even while you are working to expand those means.

Family financial management breaks down into separate, commonsense roles. The man is the breadwinner and therefore should make all the final, large-scale decisions about spending for the family—when to buy a new car, whether or not they can afford a vacation, how much to spend on new carpeting, who gets an increase in their allowance, and so on. The father should be regarded as the ultimate holder of the purse strings. Fathers, this is the essence of your duty as provider. It is an evil to force your family to depend on others for their financial survival. You must make wise, sound, far-seeing financial decisions.

The woman is the day-to-day financial monitor, the bookkeeper of the household. She is the one who tracks how much groceries cost, who spends what on school lunches, how much it costs to fill the car's tank with gasoline and so on. Because women are intimately involved with all the little transactions that take place each day, they are perfectly suited to be the accountants of the family. The wife and mother provides information to her husband, the family Chief Financial Officer. He then makes the final call on what is spent and why.

This system requires you to live within your means. That means not debt-financing your possessions and craving the material things that will not bring you joy or spiritual fulfillment. It means thinking about the future and spending wisely, always planning for tomorrow while getting what you must have today. Some very smart ways to make this happen in your family:

- Pay cash whenever possible. If you don't have it, don't buy it. Credit cards are for emergencies only.
- Buy a house if you don't already own one. It is the best investment you will ever make.
- Watch what *The Automatic Millionaire* author David Bach calls your "Latte Factor." That is, what small purchases do you make every day without thinking about them, like a coffee or newspaper, that could add up to costing you thousands of dollars a year?
- Set up a system to automatically take money from your paycheck each month (before taxes are taken out) and deposit it in a retirement fund.

- Make a budget and stick to it.
- Shop warehouse stores and buy in bulk to save.
- Call your credit card companies and demand a lower interest rate. If you threaten to take your account elsewhere, they will comply.
- Get rid of unused luxuries, like HD cable TV that you never watch.
- Cook and eat at home more often.

There are many, many things you can do. These are just a few. But common sense should be your guide. Not making enough money is not the problem for most families; spending too much money is. Control your spending and eliminate waste and you give God room to make good things happen in your economy.

You Must Invest Wisely

SACRED STONE #91

Married couples should use their gift of divine foresight to plan for their future.

One of the ways in which we reflect our nature as God's children is that we live simultaneously in multiple points in Time. We live in the present in our physical bodies, but we can cast our minds into the past or the future and reside there as well. We are the only beings other than God Himself to be able to peer into the future and see what will occur based on the actions we choose today. Such foresight is a divine gift.

It's sad then that so many married couples fail to use this gift in planning their lives for the future. I refer to the importance of investing for your financial health and your retirement. Just as every family should reduce costs, simplify and use good sense in dealing with today's finances, every couple should lay the groundwork for the future they desire through prudent, opportunistic investing.

You will not always want to work. At some point, you will want to retire from working for someone else in order to pursue the life that God has ordained for you, or to start your own enterprise. How will you manage that if you have no money to live on? That is why investment is so vital for all families. There are three kinds of investing about which you should educate yourself:

1. Investing for retirement using vehicles like IRAs, SEPs, bonds and pension funds.
2. Investing for wealth through things like stocks and real estate.
3. Investing for your legacy and giving through tools such as foundations and annuities.
4. Investing for your children's futures.

SACRED STONE #92

Investing is vital for all families.

The goals of these kinds of investing are very different, of course. But all are laudable in the eyes of God. In retirement investing, you are saving money in secure investments over decades in order to have a "nest egg" to live on when you are 60 or 65 and decide to do your own thing. If you live to 90, you may have to live on your investments for 30 years! So it behooves you to invest intelligently.

Investing for wealth is more about the present, though it can still help you meet your retirement goals. Here, you are focusing on things like buying rental properties, buying stock in growing companies and the like. Chances are, you want to create more income today while building something for tomorrow. Perhaps you want to pass on a stock portfolio to your children? This kind of investing requires expert assistance.

Investing for a legacy means you might be giving to (or even starting) a foundation, or investing in an annuity that pays you a monthly income while supporting a cause close to your heart. You can even invest in mutual funds that only buy stock in companies that share your values, from serving the Christian community to protecting the environment. This is giving investing, selfless work that is blessed by God.

Finally, investing in your children could be saving money for their educations in a 529 college account, buying them savings bonds, or putting aside money in an account that they can use to buy a house when they are older. In this case, do not let your children know about your investments. It is up to you to decide when they can have what you have saved—when admitted to a four-year university, for example, or when they are married and ready to start a family.

In all cases, there are some smart investing rules you should follow:

- Enlist the help of a financial professional. You can probably find someone in your church.
- Invest for the long term. Get rich quick schemes are always frauds.
- Invest only money you don't need to deal with daily expenses.
- Invest automatically, using automatic bank withdrawals.
- Read all information and don't make a move until you're comfortable.
- Have a tax professional available to assist you with the tax implications of any investment.

Investing can make your lives and the lives of generations of family to come richer and more rewarding, as well as improving our world. Invest with wisdom and care.

SACRED STONE #93

God wants you to cast aside all visible means of support in order to reap riches in His economy.

The idea that tithing pleases God is a myth perpetuated by those who feel guilty about giving only what they have in excess. In reality, tithing gains you none of God's favor, because you are doing the minimum. It's like you're a teenager mowing the lawn but not picking up the cut grass, then holding out your hand for your paycheck. God demands more of all of us.

Tithing is important to support your church and its many services. However, if you wish to turn your giving into God's favor and gain in His economy, tithing will not avail you. As we discussed earlier, God wants you cast aside all visible means of support in order to reap riches in His economy. Remember, Jesus gave the richest reward to the women who gave all she had, even though that was very little. Why? Because she was willing to rely completely on faith as her currency.

I am not telling you to sell your home and give all the proceeds to your church, leaving your family on the street. That would be ridiculous. What I am telling you is that if you wish to truly see monumental change in your finances, give more than a tithe. Give all you can. Some of the most remarkable changes I have ever seen have come into the lives of people in my church who have received large checks and without a moment's hesitation, signed them over to my ministry. Within days, money and opportunity were flowing to them like a river, ten times and more than ten times what they had given.

Tithing is about feeling good about yourself. If you want to attract the attention and favor of God and deal in His grace, you must do more. You must give without fear and without worry about where your next opportunity is coming from. God will send it your way.

SACRED STONE #94

Teach your children the principle of saving.

Economics define a culture. A culture is only as strong as its ability to produce. The same is true of the family. If you raise your children to be financially wise, they will grow up not with a hand out, but with a hand up thanking God for their good fortune.

Every newborn should receive two certificates. The first is the birth certificate, and the second is the savings certificate. Why give a savings certificate to your children at birth? So that they know they did not come to this earth to work for money, but to put money to work for them. You see, the savings mentality begins to form on a subconscious level long before your children have put away their first penny. Before they even learn to walk or talk, you've put money away for them. Even as young children, they have savings.

When they become old enough to save for themselves, continue to teach them to save. It doesn't take a lot of money. It's not about the money when you are teaching your children—it's about instilling the principle. Two dollars a week is plenty. Teach your children to save just two dollars a week from their allowance or their babysitting money or whatever they do to earn money, and within weeks they will begin to adopt the habit of saving.

Poverty is a learned behavior that becomes an ingrained habit. If you grow up with a wealthy mindset, you will have to *learn* to be poor. Poor people have poor habits! They act poor. They spend time with poor people. They think poor. That is because they did not grow up thinking of money as something that works for them. They grew up thinking of it as something to spend. That is why poverty communicates from generation to generation like a disease! Poor habits and poor understanding of savings lead to poor reality.

Teach your children about interest, that money grows when it is saved. Share with them Benjamin Franklin's brilliant principle that "a penny saved is a penny earned." Children will want to spend their money as soon as they get it on things like candy, magazines or food with their friends. Teach your children to set something aside for savings and help them understand that by doing so, they are working. You will give them a lesson in prosperity that will last a lifetime, and that they will teach their own children.

Jesus said, "I come that you might have life and have it more abundantly." Christ is your life, and cash is your living. Of course, money isn't everything. But freedom is everything, and money buys freedom. As Solomon the wise man said in Ecclesiastes 10:19, "*A feast is made for laughter, and wine makes the life glad; but money is the answer for all things.*" Amen.

SACRED STONE #95
Teach your children the principles of giving.

Just as our children need to learn the value of saving, they also need to learn the value of giving. When we give, our gifts come back to reward us. The universe is abundant, and we contribute to that by giving to others:

"For if you give, you will get! Your gift will return to you in full and overflowing measure, pressed down, shaken together to make room for more, and running over. Whatever measure you use to give—large or small—will be used to measure what is given back to you." —(Luke 6:38)

The most fundamental rule of God's economy is simple: you get what you give. When you give God your I Am, you get what you envision. When you give Him your complete faith and make Him your currency, you get riches. When you give to others selflessly, with no thought of return or approval, you make the world better for us all. When you reach out to others with your money to bring positive change in their lives, you bring positive energy into your own.

Giving benefits us in so many ways: we feel truly uplifted, our communities are healthier, people feel bound together in a way that nothing else can achieve, and we attract good people into our lives. When you or your children give, it becomes clear that giving sets off a cascade of positive events. People come to you with opportunities. They want to help you. They want to work with you, or give you money. Giving inspires because it is part of the spirit of God, and inspiration moves human beings more powerfully than any business plan or portfolio.

Teach your children to give without thought for themselves. In the end, it is why God has put us here. In the end, giving will make them richer in money and in spirit than they or you ever thought possible.

10

Creating a Legacy

"For I know the plans I have for you," declares the Lord, "plans to prosper you and not to harm you, plans to give you hope and a future."

—Jeremiah 29:11

God is indeed a god of generations, and we must honor Him by living beyond the present moment to a life that touches generations well into the future. Strive to make your life more than a distant memory or a name that cannot be remembered by your grandchildren. Even hundreds of years from now, when you have long since gone home to the Lord, your legacy will continue on and be remembered. Ensure that the seeds you have planted bloom for generations to come.

SACRED STONE #96
You must create a legacy for your family.

A legacy is what ensures you will make a mark upon the earth. Every parent should strive to build a legacy that will be heartily embraced by their children and their children's community—even by the entire community—for decades to come. A legacy does much: helps secure your children's future, gives you and them honor in the eyes of others, enriches your community and makes life easier for others who perhaps did not have as much as you had.

How do you leave a legacy? You must ensure the generation following you will be empowered to build upon the foundation you have laid. The Bible tells us this: *A good man leaves an inheritance to his children and his children's children. —(Proverbs 13:22).* That means more than leaving money or material possessions to your children after you die. It means creating a bulwark of good works and financial security while you are alive that give your children the freedom and inspiration to continue your work of changing the world in their own way.

There many kinds of legacies. Some fathers leave their children inheritances that can only be claimed if certain conditions are met. Others launch organizations that feed and clothe the needy so their children can follow in their footsteps. Still others create great works that their children can take over and continue to build upon, like the children of a great author protecting his works after his death. This chapter is concerned with all those types of legacies, but let's begin with the financial.

SACRED STONE #97

You must have life insurance.

As we have discussed, fathers are thinkers and planners. They understand that death is inevitable and use wisely the life God has given them to prepare for the next generation to come. One of the best ways to do this is to purchase life insurance.

Hold on just a minute, you say. I don't even want to think about my death. Or maybe you don't believe you should pay your hard-earned money into a life insurance policy now just to make someone else rich when you die. The simple truth is, after your death, you will go on to be with God in the realm of Spirit. Money will mean nothing to you, but your offspring will remain in the material realm and money will be a necessary part of their lives. This is a need all fathers should and must attend to.

Not having life insurance is foolish. Those who avoid buying life insurance because they don't want to acknowledge their own mortality are ruled by fear instead of by love. Life is not the opposite of death; love is its opposite. But fear of death grips the hearts and they cannot see that by buying life insurance, they are not acknowledging their own death, but instead acknowledging the lives of their heirs.

SACRED STONE #98

Life insurance allows you to be a blessing to your family even after your death, rather than a burden.

Nobody likes to talk about dying, but it is something all of us will do. Just as there is life, there must be death. That is the way God created the universe. Without death, there would be no change, no passion within us to live our lives to the fullest. Death is a natural, holy part of the scheme of existence. Let me tell you that death is nothing to fear. Dying may be unpleasant (depending on how it occurs), but we know that we are not the bodies we inhabit; they are mere shells for the aware Spirit within us. So death is not the end of existence, but it is the end of our existence in this reality. Does it not make more sense to acknowledge mortality and give a loving gift to those who will remain in this material plane? We will have no use for money, but they will.

Life insurance does not expedite death. Filling out a policy does not mean you will die any sooner. What it *does* is allow you to be a blessing to your family even after your death, rather than a burden. It gives you the power to create a memorial to yourself for future generations to remember you as a wise and thinking individual who planned for the end of his life as well as the continuation of the lives of his heirs. Too many churches in our communities have to bury members who did not purchase life insurance, and then help care for their families as well. It takes a prosperous mindset to understand that life insurance is not a way of making someone else rich after your death, but of safeguarding future generations and building a legacy.

Life insurance can help you while you are alive and well, too. You can borrow against it to help your children go to college, buy a home or pay for other expenses. You can use it to benefit your children *now* as well as when you die.

As a father, how much insurance do you need? A good rule of thumb is to purchase life insurance in the amount of seven times your present income. Any less, and you are underinsured. If you earn $40,000 a year, you should have $280,000 *minimum* in life insurance. This is enough money to allow your survivors to keep the roof over their heads, grieve without worrying about paying the bills, and create good works in your memory.

What if you have more than your future generations need? Make a donation to your community hospital, church, or a charity that you support. Have a hospital program or charitable fund set up in your name. Leave an offering that speaks long after your physical being has ceased to do so. Giving to others, an aspect of humanity that comes directly from God, can continue long after you are gone from this world.

SACRED STONE #99

Instill respect for your name.

No matter what you gain or lose in life, you will always have your name. This is why we must instill in our children the value of their name, so that they will forever respect and guard it.

Names are vibrations from the first letter to the last. They are your body, soul and spirit. Your first name represents your physical body, your middle name represents your soul, and your last name represents your spirit. Jordan, Thompson, Jackson—all of these are spiritual identities. They symbolize the spirit of your home and your family.

This is especially important to instill in your sons. Your daughters will grow up, get married and take another man's name, but your sons will carry on your name forever. My sons will be Jordans forever. I tell them all the time, "Don't ruin my name. My name is my spirit. Protect our name and you protect our spirit."

A good name is more desirable than great riches. —(Proverbs 22:1)

In African culture, they'll take on the name of an individual who is deceased to keep that spirit and continuity going from one generation to the next. Names have power. Names can move mountains. The reputation attached to the name of a person can compel others to give great sums of money, perform seemingly impossible deeds, offer incredible kindnesses, or open doors that would otherwise remain closed. That is how political dynasties work. Names and reputations are priceless and must be protected.

What abut people who have several middle names? Just as you can have many levels of incarnation in the soul, you can have many middle names. When I was preparing to become ordained in the church, my mother had no middle name for me. Bishop Roy Brown said I had to have a middle name, and when he went into spirit the only middle name he could come up with was Elijah, like the prophet Elijah.

Names are sacred. It is a shame that we have lost the naming ceremonies that were so revered by our ancestors. We no longer give our children names that have meaning and purpose; instead, we just assign the most popular names of the moment, or we name our children after celebrities and athletes. Give your children meaningful names and discuss the meaning with them, so that they have an understanding of who they are meant to be. You can find such names in the Bible, but that is not the only source. Look in the great literature of your culture, such as great African tribal names. Take names from literature as inspiration. Just be certain that the names bear a weight of deep, personal meaning. Names are a story. What story are your children's names telling? If you have no children yet, what will the names of your unborn children reveal?

SACRED STONE #100

Teach your children to seek meaning by asking questions.

When I see a young man with a thumb ring, I ask him to tell me the meaning of his jewelry. Most of the time, he will shrug and tell me it is just jewelry—one of his friends had one and he liked it so he got one for himself. But he has no idea what it means. Well, the thumb is the strongest finger on the hand. It is not made for a ring; when you wear a thumb ring, you bind your will.

Here's another example: Everywhere you look, you see kids with their pants hanging down around their hips or even their knees. They don't wear belts because they like having their pants falling off their bodies. I asked one of them, "Why are your pants hanging down around your ankles?" He told me, "It's just a look. They can't wear belts in jail." I just shook my head. I thought, OK, so you're dressing for where you want to be going? That's messed up. We need these kids to really stop and ask themselves, do I *want* to be going to jail? Why am I dressing like this?

Teach your children to seek *meaning*—to question the actions of others rather than just blindly following them. Remember the story I told you about my great-grandmother cutting off both ends of the ham? For fifty years, no one questioned why the women in our family did that. When someone finally did question it, we learned how foolish we were for continuing to do it. You have to seek meaning and ask questions. When you ask questions, you learn. When you learn, you grow.

We need to teach our children to ask questions without worrying about looking stupid or ignorant. Life is filled with educated people. Teach your children to value the opportunity to learn, and to question every educated person they meet. All acts have significance. Everything we do, from what we eat for breakfast to the music we listen to, guides us in a direction toward something. Will that something be a blessing or curse? Will it enrich or impoverish us? When children know to look for meaning and context every day of their lives, they will know more about their journey—and be able to make smart decisions about the people and choices that enter their lives.

SACRED STONE #101

*Make sure your family is
continually growing.*

Every living thing is oriented toward growth. Plants, animals, people—we are all meant to continually grow, change, and prosper. You cannot achieve the next level of growth if you simply aim to survive. When growth is absent, retardation is present.

We hear a great deal about the importance of economic growth, whether it's at the scale of a single company or a national economy. That is because growth is the opposite of stagnation. When a public company fails to show revenue growth, its stock plummets. When a country's economic activity does not grow, it is said to be in recession. Without growth, there is death. When something fails to grow, whether it is an economy or a family, it is beginning to stagnate and rot. We must always be moving forward and expanding in wisdom, prosperity, love and awareness of God.

Strive to keep your family growing. I don't mean increasing the size of your family. I'm talking about developing your family's strength, intellect, love and potential. Take on challenges as a family. Help one another through difficult times. Take risks if the rewards are great enough. Growth only happens when you take a chance and go out beyond your comfort zone. The key to success is ability to venture into the darkness and trust God to show you the way.

How is your family growing? As we bring this journey together to a close, ask yourself these questions as a kind of Family Growth Self Test:

i.   Who is the final source of discipline and decision-making in your household?

ii. Do you and your spouse each accept and abide by the God-ordained roles you are each to fill in your family?

iii. Does the husband and father in the family grasp and execute his duties?

iv. Does the wife and mother in the family grasp and execute her duties?

v.   Do you both put your relationship first? If not, how can you improve?

vi. How do you ensure there is trust and communication between you and your spouse at all times?

vii. What rules must your children follow?

viii. Do the boys in your family understand what is expected of them as young men? Do you expose them to male company often?

ix. Do the girls in your family understand what is expected of them as young women? Do you expose them to female influence often?

x. How do you, your spouse and your children communicate? Resolve conflict? Does it work?

xi. How have you made space and time for God in your family?

xii. How have you made the church a part of your children's lives?

xiii. What steps are you taking to ensure financial security for yourselves and your children?

xiv. How does your family give back?

xv. What are you doing to create a legacy?

Once you know the answers, sit down with your spouse and discuss them. If changes are called for, make them or seek the counsel of a prophet or other church leader to help you decide what to do. It is never too late to change the course of your family, to bring it into the light of maturity, richness, discipline, vision, spirituality and love that emanates from God.

About The Author

Bishop E. Bernard Jordan is nothing less than a modern day prophet. In 1989 he predicted the 2005 Gulf Coast natural disaster, storm Katrina that had a devastating effect on the people in New Orleans. Sought after by nations of the world for his accurate prophecies, Jordan has prophesied the word of the Lord to literally millions of people. He is noted for his uncanny accuracy of the prophecies that he ministers. Businessmen, political officials, celebrities and churches are numbered among the thousands who have consulted Bishop Jordan for counsel and direction through the Word of the Lord.

The Master Prophet has traveled to Swaziland, South Africa, and delivered the Word of the Lord to the Queen and the Royal Family. He has prophesied in many nations, including Germany, Canada, Korea and the Caribbean, bringing an astute word of counsel to the leadership and royalty of those countries. In February 1988, he was invited to address a special assembly of ambassadors and diplomats at the United Nations concerning the oppressive racism in South Africa. He addressed the assembly again in February 1992, and prophesied of the impending liberation of South Africa, which has come to pass.

He has been featured on NBC's Today Show, FOX 5, Good Day New York, CNN, and many, many others. He was also featured in The Daily News, New York Times, New York Post and Newsday with some of his congregates as well as in an interview in Billboard Magazine on his views concerning social issues. His life-changing messages on reformation and liberation have sparked acclaim, as well as controversy, as he teaches the unadulterated Word of God.

He is the founder of Zoë Ministries in New York City, a prophetic gathering with a vision to impact the globe with Christ's message of liberation.

Bishop Jordan has written more than 40 books including best-sellers, Mentoring, Spiritual Protocol, What Every Woman Should Know About Men, The Power of Money, and Cosmic Economics, and New York Times Bestseller, The Laws of Thinking: 20 Secrets to Using The Divine Power of Your Mind To Manifest Prosperity. He holds his Doctorate in Religious Studies and a Ph.D. in Religious Studies. He and his wife Pastor Debra have five children. You can watch him live on television on The Power of Prophecy telecast or through live streaming, just visit his site at www.bishopjordan.com.

For Further Reading
by Bishop E. Bernard Jordan:

The Business of Getting Rich: 12 Secrets to Unveiling The Spiritual Side of Wealth In You

Cosmic Economics: The Universal Keys To Wealth

Dreams & Visions: Letters from God and How To Read Them!

Prophetic Congress: Deep Calleth Unto Deep

Prophetic Congress: The Summit Volume II

Prophetic Genesis

School of the Prophets Volume I

School of the Prophets Volume II

Spiritual Protocol

Unveiling The Mysteries

The Laws of Thinking: 20 Secrets to Using the Divine Power of Your Mind to Manifest Prosperity

The Marital Union of Thought

The Science of Prophecy

From Pastor Debra A. Jordan:

Prophetic Reflections: Poetry From the Heart of the Prophetess

FREE

WRITTEN PROPHECY

As seen on TV !

To get your free personal written word
in the mail from me,
Master Prophet E. Bernard Jordan,
simply visit our site at
www.bishopjordan.com
and follow the prompts.

The Master Prophet will see the Mind of God
on your behalf and he will give you the
ANSWERS YOU HAVE BEEN SEEKING.